Work Issues

ISSUES

Volume 107

Editor

Craig Donnellan

First published by Independence
PO Box 295
Cambridge CB1 3XP
England

British Library Cataloguing in Publication Data
Work Issues – (Issues Series)
I. Donnellan, Craig II. Series
306.3'6

ISBN 1 86168 327 8

Printed in Great Britain
MWL Print Group Ltd

Typeset by
Lisa Firth

Cover
The illustration on the front cover is by
Pumpkin House.

CONTENTS

Chapter One: Work in the UK Today

Job satisfaction?	1
The joy of work?	2
Auf wiedersehen, pet?	3
Unprepared, uninformed and unsure of success	4
Do you work for a tyrant or a pussycat?	5
UK employees working longest hours in Europe	6
Sicknote culture?	6
'Sicknote Britain' an urban myth, says TUC report	8
Pride and prejudice blur men's view of the glass cliff	9
Losing your job is 'worse than losing a loved one'	10
Work this way	11

Chapter Two: The Work-Life Balance

Workers in 30s suffer most from work-life imbalance	14
The time and the place . . .	14
Flexibility for parents	16
Work-life balance in the British economy	16
Part-time and flexible working	17
Flexible working can keep your absence rates healthy	18
Flexible working	19
What are working from home and teleworking?	19
Becoming a working parent	21

Working from home	22
Work and childcare	23
Facts about working dads	24
Mothers on the run	26
Arranging a grown-up gap year	27
Working hard?	28
Are you a workaholic?	29

Chapter Three: Work and Young People

Young people at work	30
The skills gap	31
Skills shortage 12-year high	33
Job crisis for school leavers	33
Business welcomes education white paper	34
Is it really worth it?	35
Modern Apprenticeships	36
Youth unemployment at all-time high	37
Key Facts	40
Additional Resources	41
Index	42
Acknowledgements	44

Introduction

Work Issues is the one hundred and seventh volume in the **Issues** series. The aim of this series is to offer up-to-date information about important issues in our world.

Work Issues looks at employment in the UK today, maintaining a work-life balance, and work and young people.

The information comes from a wide variety of sources and includes:
Government reports and statistics
Newspaper reports and features
Magazine articles and surveys
Website material
Literature from lobby groups
and charitable organisations.

It is hoped that, as you read about the many aspects of the issues explored in this book, you will critically evaluate the information presented. It is important that you decide whether you are being presented with facts or opinions. Does the writer give a biased or an unbiased report? If an opinion is being expressed, do you agree with the writer?

Work Issues offers a useful starting-point for those who need convenient access to information about the many issues involved. However, it is only a starting-point. At the back of the book is a list of organisations which you may want to contact for further information.

*****

Job satisfaction?

Not much for Britain's hard slog 'robot' workers

Having to work harder and act like 'robots', with little scope for personal initiative, are the chief reasons for declining job satisfaction in Britain, according to new research sponsored by the ESRC.

Feelings of insecurity, too high expectations and people being 'over-educated' and unable to find work to match their qualifications, are largely dismissed as factors, in the study led by Professor Francis Green of the University of Kent.

His team found no evidence to back suggestions that the dull mood of workers may be due to successive generations having ever higher expectations from their jobs and being disappointed by the realities of employment.

The investigation, which also looked at other European countries and the United States, signals a falling sense of well-being among both British and German workers, but admits defeat when it comes to explaining the decline in Germany.

In Britain, between 1972 and 1983 there was a small downward trend in average job satisfaction. There is a lack of data for much of the 1980s, but during the 1990s, three separate sources show significant declines.

Average job satisfaction also fell in West Germany between 1984 and 1997, after which it recovered slightly until 2000. Immediately after re-unification, East Germans had very much lower job satisfaction than workers in West Germany, but the gap narrowed within a couple of years. After 1994, however, East Germans settled also into a decline, in line with the rest of the country.

The study found a modest downward movement in the Netherlands over 1994-2000 and in Finland over 1996-2000, yet in neither case is it

significant, nor is there any notable trend elsewhere in Europe.

In the US, there was a small downward trend in job satisfaction from 1972 to 2002. But the figures suggests that even over 100 years, it would only fall by 0.1 points – not much on a possible range of 1 to 4.

Professor Green said: 'The most satisfied employee is one who is in a secure job, with a high level of individual discretion and participation in decision-making, but not requiring highly intensive work effort. They will be well-matched to their job in terms of both qualifications and hours of work, be well-paid but have relatively low pay expectations.'

Professor Green continued: 'In Britain, all of the fall in overall job satisfaction between 1992 and 2001 could be accounted for by people having less personal responsibility and use of initiative in their work, combined with an increase in the effort required.

'It was implausible to blame job insecurity, because over this period unemployment had fallen and other evidence suggested a falling sense of insecurity during the latter part of the 1990s.'

His report adds that whilst there had been a small increase in people unable to find work to match their qualifications, this was far too small to account for the effect on job satisfaction.

In Germany through most of the 1990s, the fear of job loss was increasing, unsurprisingly given the rise of unemployment throughout that period, and insecurity partly accounts for the decline in job satisfaction. But, says the study, when the whole period 1984 to 1998 is analysed, job insecurity cannot explain the downward trend.

Professor Green said: 'In short, the case of Germany remains a puzzle. We could find nothing in the data we examined which could account for the decline there.'

■ The above information is from the Economic and Social Research Council – see page 41 for address details.

© ESRC 2005

The joy of work?

Information from the Work Foundation

- The UK has a three-tier labour market. Two-thirds of UK workers seem to be enjoying the good life, being satisfied or very satisfied with their work. But over 4 million workers, 15% of the total workforce, are dissatisfied or very dissatisfied with their jobs. These people tend to work in low skill parts of the economy, often with little or no control over when and where they work and with little say in how they work. But those suffering most from a well-being deficit are the unemployed and economically inactive who want a job. Their life satisfaction is only just over half that of those in work or caring for others.

- Working for yourself makes you happy: more than 80% of the self-employed are satisfied or very satisfied with their jobs, while 67% of part-timers and 64% of full-timers say they are satisfied with work. Efforts to make it easier to set up in business and stay in business, minimising 'red tape' where it harms rather than helps, are good for people's well-being as well as the economy.

- Married workers seem the most satisfied with divorced and separated people the least satisfied.

- Work is very important to well-being especially for those who are in control of what they do. For everyone children and partners are the most important elements of happiness. But work is as important as spending time with friends or spending time on leisure.

- Hours matter. Despite relatively high levels of satisfaction with their job, a majority 61% want to work fewer hours – 70% of men and 52% of women.

- It seems that going down the pub or playing sport is significantly more important to men (49%) than spending time with their kids (20%), friends (20%) or partners (22%).

- But over two million people suffer from work-lust. These 'workophiles' far prefer being at work to being at home. For them work/life balance is for other people – in their world the 'workophobes'.

- The UK's long hours problem is a well-paid problem. Income follows hours with 1 in 5 of those earning £60,000 working more than 60 hours a week. Those earning between £46,000 and £51,000 a year have nearly 70% of their number working up to 60 hours a week and 7.7% working more than that.

- However, over 400,000 workers are genuine wage slaves, earning less than £16,000 a year for working more than 60 hours a week. Tougher enforcement of the minimum wage legislation is clearly required in many of these cases.

- It is also clear that the UK has an aspirations gap, with only 53% of respondents agreeing that job satisfaction is of critical importance to why they do their job. In addition nearly 50% are very happy with their levels of remuneration which is good news for organisational pay setters.

Working for yourself makes you happy: more than 80% of the self-employed are satisfied or very satisfied with their jobs

---

- Most workers like control over when and where they work. Flexible working practices that currently cover a fifth of the workforce need to be expanded. The Government's right to request flexible working should be extended as rapidly as possible to all workers – provided businesses can have some say over whether it works.

- Employers need to re-invent job security. Whilst job tenure has stayed roughly the same, people do not feel secure. When restructuring, the first element should be to look at how to minimise the effects on the existing workforce, redeploying and re-training as necessary.

- The above information is the executive summary of *The joy of work?* report published by the Work Foundation. To view the entire PDF, visit www.theworkfoundation.com or see page 41 for address details.

© The Work Foundation

Auf wiedersehen, pet?

Manpower reveals 8 in 10 workers would work abroad

Some 82% of Brits would consider working abroad, according to research released today (25 August 2004) by Manpower, the UK's leading recruitment company.

With summer drawing to a close, Manpower has conducted research to find out whether people would think about working in a foreign country and which working practices from other European countries people would most like Britain to adopt.

It seems that for many people their holiday abroad gives them a taste for more – almost a third of the 813 people surveyed said they'd like 25 days' minimum annual leave, like our Austrian counterparts. A further 27% would like to adopt the French working style of a 35-hour maximum working week.

Hazel Detsiny, director at Manpower, says: 'Many people travel during the summer, often giving them an insight into the work cultures of our European neighbours. With the recent EU expansion there has been increased awareness of the possibilities of working abroad. However, people should remember that foreign working might not be plain sailing: people have to overcome language and cultural barriers, have to make new friends and get used to new ways of working – it's not a decision to be taken lightly.'

The research also shows that a sleepy 19% of those surveyed would most like to see Spanish-style afternoon siestas introduced to their working environment and a further 17% would choose to have 14 bank holidays a year, like in Portugal.

People are travelling abroad more than ever, exposing them to different work practices and cultures

---

Hazel continues: 'People are travelling abroad more than ever, exposing them to different work practices and cultures. The results of this survey show that employees are interested in alternative work practices. Employers need to be flexible in their approach when putting together benefits packages and looking at motivating employees.'

■ The above information is from Manpower – see page 41 for address details or visit www.manpower.co.uk.

© Manpower 2004

Notes

813 people were surveyed in an online poll. The results are as follows:

Which of the following working practices from these holiday destinations would you most like for the UK?
■ Afternoon siestas, like in Spain: 19%
■ 14 bank holidays a year, like in Portugal: 17%
■ A maximum 35-hour working week, like in France: 27%
■ 25 days' minimum annual leave, like in Austria: 30%
■ Parental leave entitlement of 66 weeks, like in Denmark: 7%

Would you consider working in a foreign country?
■ Yes: 82%
■ No: 18%

Unprepared, uninformed and unsure of success

But the British entrepreneur is still ready to 'Risk It All' – 98% of entrepreneurs start-up without any business training

First-time entrepreneurs are continuing to make the same mistakes and begin in business with little or no adequate training or planning, according to research launched today. The research, commissioned on behalf of learndirect business, questioned entrepreneurs on their views on a range of subjects linked to the risks involved in starting up a business venture.

Perhaps most surprising was the price entrepreneurs were willing to pay in pursuit of their business dream:

- 11% said they would risk their relationship with their partner
- 26% were prepared to get into heavy debt
- 30% were willing to risk losing all their savings
- A small number, 4%, were even willing to pay the ultimate price and risk their health.

Insufficient planning obviously increases the chances of a business failing and is identified as a key issue amongst UK entrepreneurs:

- 25% of respondents felt they were unprepared before they started their own business with a further 8% suggesting they were 'very unprepared' before opening the doors for trading.

With just under 380,000 businesses closing in 2003 alone, the research revealed a worrying statistic. 98% of respondents had never undertaken any business training before starting up in business.

Despite the stress and risks involved, being a successful entrepreneur still has numerous benefits:

- 75% of respondents suggesting that being your own boss is the number one reason for running your own business.
- Followed by 17% enjoying the greater work-life balance it gave...
- ...and lastly 7% of respondents citing the share of the profits it gave them.

Learndirect business spokeswoman Sarah Turpin, head of workforce development and policy, urges entrepreneurs not to 'Risk It All', but rather invest in business training early on: 'The research findings demonstrate that this country's entrepreneurial spirit is alive and well. Unfortunately what it also demonstrates is the unnecessary risks those entrepreneurs are still willing to take. The relatively small costs involved with undertaking business training could prove to be critical in saving a business in the long run. We must continue to emphasise the importance of education and training to build a long-term sustainable business.'

75% of respondents, currently running their own businesses, now realise the importance of training

and agreed with the statement that they would be interested in attending first-time or refresher courses. Also, the importance of training in hindsight is not lost on existing entrepreneurs, with 91% now agreeing they could improve their business through education and training.

75% of respondents suggested that being your own boss is the number one reason for running your own business

---

Turpin continues: 'Through government initiatives such as learndirect business, business training is now easily accessible, through our Premier Business Centres and/or over the internet. We continue to ensure our courses are really relevant to the entrepreneur, giving practical training and education in areas such as financial planning, IT, compliance issues and sales and marketing. We recognise that any form of training must meet the needs of business'

The learndirect business research demonstrates the lack of importance new entrepreneurs give to business training and education and may go some way to explaining why so many new businesses struggle to get off the ground.

- The above information is reprinted with kind permission from Ufi – please visit www.ufi.com for more information or if you would like to write to them, see page 41 for address details.

© *Ufi, June 2004*

Do you work for a tyrant or a pussycat?

The industry you work in could determine your boss's type

The boss from hell may be a dying breed, according to new research from Lloyds TSB and Working Families who are searching for the UK's Best Boss 2005. Two-fifths (39 per cent) of Brits say their boss is just a 'Pussycat' at heart compared to one-fifth (21 per cent) who are working for a 'Tyrant'.

Lloyds TSB and Working Families, organisers of the Britain's Best Boss awards, have analysed the management styles of different bosses and identified four boss types: the Tyrant, the Pussycat, the Entertainer, and the Leader.

Notes

Respondents were asked to identify their boss among the following boss types:

The Tyrant
Dictatorial and ruthless, favouring short-term gains over long-term success, putting profit before people.

The Pussycat
Tries hard to be an effective leader but doesn't always get it right, letting their heart rule their head too often.

The Entertainer
More interested in being an entertainer and everyone's best friend, than an effective leader.

The Leader
Inspiring and motivational, encouraging teamwork, relationship-building and the personal development of staff.

1703 people were surveyed by tickbox.net in March 2005

Encouragingly, a third (32 per cent) of those surveyed put their boss in the 'Leader' category, viewing their boss as inspiring, motivational and concerned with the well-being of their staff. However, according to the UK's workforce, it would appear bosses' management styles vary widely depending on the industry they work in.

Transport bosses are more likely to be ruthless 'Tyrants' who put profit before people, with 32 per cent of bosses being put into this category compared to a national average of 21 per cent. Bosses from the IT and Telecoms industries are ten times more likely to adopt a David Brent-like style and be the 'Entertainer' compared to Media bosses (12 per cent compared to 1 per cent) who are more likely to be pushovers and fall into the management category of Pussycats. But it's good news for those who work in Retail, with more retail workers (38 per cent) classing their boss as an effective 'Leader' who values their staff than any other industry.

Fiona Cannon, head of equality and diversity at Lloyds TSB, said: 'It's great news for so many people view their boss as a true leader who cares about their employees. One of the keys to being a good boss is to recognise and understand the importance of work-life balance and that's exactly the type of manager that we're searching for to claim the title of Britain's Best Boss 2005.'

Two-fifths (39 per cent) of Brits say their boss is just a 'Pussycat' at heart compared to one-fifth (21 per cent) who are working for a 'Tyrant'

Sarah Jackson, Working Families, said: 'We know that managers who have found work-life balance works for their teams are the best persuaders of their peers. It's already clear that employees around the country really appreciate bosses who help them to balance their responsibilities at work and at home.'

■ The above information is from Working Families – see page 41 for their address details.

© Working Families 2005

UK employees working longest hours in Europe

UK workers are continuing to put in longer hours than almost all of their European counterparts, according to a new report

The UK now has the second highest proportion of men working more than 60 hours per week in the EU, with Ireland the highest.

Equally worrying, according to the independent research organisation the Work Foundation, is the culture of 'presenteeism' – of employees spending ever longer hours at work because they think it is expected of them – that is becoming engrained in the workplace.

The findings add fuel to UNISON's work-life balance campaign, which is attempting to address the increasing demands of employers on their workforce.

The report *Still at Work?* examines all 15 EU countries, including workers in all major occupation groups, industry sectors and socio-economic groups.

While the actual proportion of people working more than 60 hours per week in any one European country is still small, the report shows that in the UK around 896,000 men and 492,000 women regularly do so.

Administrators and skilled manual workers are among those more commonly working long hours, with those in the private sector more so than in the public sector.

'Long hours cultures can have real implications for each country,' said Dr Marc Cowling, chief economist of the Work Foundation and one of the authors of the report. 'They can lead to an increase in workplace stress, and a decline in productivity, as marginal productivity decreases with the number of hours worked.'

UNISON's work-life balance campaign aims to:
■ make sure that work-life balance issues are an integral part of the bargaining and negotiating process with employers;
■ provide branch activists and members with information and resources to highlight the issues, the benefits and best practice;
■ put pressure on the government to introduce incentives – and possibly legislation – to create a worker-friendly approach to working hours, and to ensure equality in the provision of flexible working opportunities.

■ The above information is from UNISON, Britain's biggest trade union – visit www.unison.org.uk for more or see page 41 for address details.
© UNISON 2005

Sicknote culture?

Workplace absence has increased for the first time in five years, adding an extra ten million days to a problem that cost business £11.6bn last year alone

A survey of over 500 firms by the Confederation of British Industry (CBI) and AXA, shows that over three-quarters of companies suspect employees of taking 'unwarranted' long weekends by calling in sick on Fridays or Mondays.

Seventy-eight per cent of organisations said there was either a definite or possible link between patterns of absence and the unauthorised extension of the weekend.

The annual survey also reveals that employers fear 25 million days were lost last year through staff taking non-genuine sickness absence or 'pulling sickies'. That accounts for 15% of all absence at a cost of £1.75bn.

The total number of working days lost to absence has increased for the first time since 1998, caused by an eight per cent rise in service sector absence. Total days lost rose from 166 million in 2002 to 176 million in 2003. That is 7.2 days per employee, an increase of six per cent or almost half a day.

The cost of overall workplace absence remains worryingly high, with firms paying £11.6bn in 2003 to cover the salaries of absent individuals and the resulting overtime and temporary cover. This translates to £475 per employee and matches the overall figure in last year's survey.

'Pulling sickies'

John Cridland, CBI Deputy Director General, said: 'Firms understand that the majority of absence is due to genuine minor sickness. But absence is a serious and expensive concern that is on the increase. This rise has been caused by a growing level of service sector absence that may be the direct result of the tough year endured by the sector. As costs rose in 2003, many services firms were forced to slim down and conduct the same amount of work with fewer staff. This would have increased pressure on employees and possibly affected morale, leading to an increase in absence.

'Unwarranted long weekends and staff "pulling sickies" are taking their toll on the UK's ability to absorb the enormous cost of absence. With employees "pulling sickies" adding £1.75bn to last year's absence bill, companies will be concerned about staff awarding themselves days off during this Summer's Euro 2004 football tournament.'

The gap between public and private sector absence is worryingly large, with public sector staff taking an average of two extra sick days than their private sector counterparts. Public sector absence averaged 8.9 days a year and cost £566 per employee, significantly higher than private sector absence which averaged 6.9 days and cost £450 per employee.

The CBI points to figures showing that the public sector accounts for 29 per cent of total UK employment but public sector absence accounted for 36 per cent of total absence. That is 64 million days of the total 176 million days lost to absence.

The CBI says that the UK taxpayer would be saved £1bn if public sector absence was brought in line with the private sector average. Overall public sector absence cost a total of £4bn last year.

Firms said that long-term absence accounted for just five per cent of all absence cases but was responsible for a third of total time lost through absence.

The survey also shows manufacturing firms reported higher absence levels than service sector companies – 7.4 days lost compared with 6.4 days lost. Service sector absence increased by eight per cent – or half a day – in this survey, rising from 5.9 days in last year's survey.

Absence

Absence varied greatly across the UK but this survey has consistently shown no lasting link between absence and region. Absence was highest in the north-west (10.1 days), followed by the east and north of England (both 8.1 days) and Northern Ireland (8 days). Average absence levels were recorded in Wales (7.8 days), the east midlands (7.3), southern England (7), south-west and south-east England (both 6.9)

and the west midlands (6.6). The lowest absence levels were recorded in Yorkshire & Humberside (6.3), Greater London (6) and Scotland (5.6).

Manual workers have significantly higher absence rates than non-manual employees. Manual worker rates averaged 8.7 days per employee in 2003, compared with 5.9 days per employee for non-manual staff.

Larger organisations reported higher absence levels than smaller ones. Firms employing over 5000 averaged 10.2 days per employee, while companies with less than 50 staff averaged 4.2 days. The CBI believes smaller firms have lower absence rates because of more frequent senior management contact and greater peer pressure.

Dudley Lusted, AXA Head of Corporate Healthcare Development, said: 'Absence is a two-headed monster. Short-term absence responds well to good people management as the causes often have a lot to do with employees' attitudes towards work. But an altogether different approach is required for managing long-term absence, which, whilst small in number, accounts for a third of working time lost. That more companies are introducing rehabilitation policies is welcome recognition that doing nothing is not a viable option. Early intervention and active management are key to success, as evidenced by the finding that companies that provided long-term sick employees with access to medical care or treatments had lower absence levels.'

■ The above information is from Working Balance – for more visit www.workingbalance.co.uk.

© *Working Balance*

Cake doesn't cut it

Manpower reveals what makes an ideal colleague

Nearly 40% of British workers say reliability is the ultimate quality in a co-worker, according to research released today (30 Sept 2004) by Manpower, the UK's leading recruitment company.

As part of Manpower's search for Britain's most valued employee in the workplace, the company has conducted research to find out what type of colleague people most want to work with.

It seems us Brits will not tolerate being let down by office slackers: 39% of the 1,187 people surveyed said their ideal colleague would be a Reliable Richard – that dependable colleague who's always on time and never misses a deadline. Conversely, Suck-up Sarahs need to rethink their position in the office popularity stakes: despite being regular providers of teas, coffees, cakes and treats, these eager-to-please colleagues would only be chosen by 1% as the ideal co-worker.

Straight-talking, honest colleagues came second in the poll, receiving one-fifth of the votes, closely followed, with 18% of the votes, by colleagues who are willing to put in extra effort to help out, for example by working through a lunch hour or staying after 5pm.

And there's bad news for David Brent wannabes (of BBC's *The Office*) – the office clown was the ideal colleague of only 12% of voters. The survey also shows that just one in ten workers rate the agony aunt who provides the shoulder to cry on as the ideal colleague.

Comments Charles Ashworth, director at Manpower UK: 'Good co-workers are fundamental to our happiness in our jobs. A colleague who injects laughter into the workplace is always a "nice to have" but being able to rely on a colleague to deliver on promises and not slack off is clearly far more important. We depend on our colleagues to fulfil their work commitments so that we in turn can fulfil our own.'

■ The above information is from Manpower's website which can be found at www.manpower.co.uk, or see page 41 for address details.

© *Manpower 2004*

'Sicknote Britain' an urban myth, says TUC report

Information from UNISON

A new report published today (7 Jan 2005) by the TUC counters the myth of 'sicknote Britain', including the idea that public sector workers throw more 'sickies' than anyone else.

Sicknote Britain also contradicts the assertions that stress is not a serious illness, and that the solution to damaging levels of sick leave is a cutback on the numbers of people in receipt of incapacity benefit.

A very real problem identified by the report is the number of people who struggle into work when they are genuinely ill – which can affect their co-workers and lead to long-term sickness.

'When employers complain of sicknote Britain, they are attacking some of Europe's most loyal employees,' said TUC general secretary Brendan Barber. '"Sicknote Britain" is an urban myth.'

As if to underline this view, another TUC report earlier this week revealed that UK workers did unpaid overtime in 2004 that would have amounted to an extra £4,650 each, had they been paid for their efforts.

Agreeing with the findings of *Sicknote Britain*, UNISON called for improved methods of 'monitoring and managing absence', so that work-related causes of absence could be identified and tackled.

Rather than Britain being a nation of malingerers, the report shows that:

- British workers are less likely to take short-term time off sick than in any European country except Denmark;
- only Austria, Germany and Ireland lose less working time due to long-term absence;
- the average period lost by a private sector worker through short-term absence is 5.5 days, compared to 4.9 by a public sector worker;
- the number of people on Incapacity Benefit is on the decrease;
- a majority of employers accept that most staff time taken off ill is because of genuine sickness;
- 75% of workers confess to having struggled into work when they were actually too ill to do so.

While public sector workers tend to be accused of throwing more 'sickies' than other workers, says the report, the statistics show that employees who take the 'odd day or two' off work are more often found in the private sector.

Longer-term absence is more common amongst public sector workers but, the report says, this is inextricably linked to the more stressful nature of many jobs in the sector.

It also attacks commentators who suggest that many people who are off work with stress are not really that ill. It states that the symptoms suffered by stressed-out employees are serious – including mental health and chronic physical health problems.

The report concludes that employers who are serious about reducing levels of sickness absence should be looking at ways of making work more flexible, and introducing greater work/life balance into workers' daily routines.

And it identifies unions as having a key role to play in cutting sickness absence – unionised workplaces have fewer than half the number of workplace injuries than non-unionised firms – by helping employers develop family-friendly work policies and rehabilitation and return-to-work practices.

'Many of our members bend over backwards to be in work despite being ill, and they should be discouraged from doing so for all the reasons outlined in the report,' said UNISON national health and safety officer Hope Daley.

'We want employers to develop and support a culture where workers are healthy, happy and at work, and where those who are ill are encouraged to take the time they need to recover from illness, instead of being penalised for doing so.'

Workplace-related accidents and injuries were a major cause of sickness absence, Daley said, and as a first step employers should work with safety representatives to focus on ways of preventing such mishaps.

She also highlighted work-related stress as a major concern within the public sector, which would 'only worsen, if ignored by employers'. Bosses should comply with the HSE management standards on stress to reduce its prevalence.

'In short, we want to see improved methods of monitoring and managing absence, so that work-related causes of absences can be identified and tackled,' she said. 'And we want more emphasis given to rehabilitating those on sick leave.'

- The above information is from UNISON's website which can be found at www.unison.org.uk, or see page 41 for address details.

© Unison 2005

Pride and prejudice blur men's view of the glass cliff

Information from the Economic and Social Research Council

Accepting a fact as scientific is not a simple matter of whether the methodology is sound – what matters is whether the science that underpins it is compatible with our stereotypes and prejudices.

That is the key finding of a new study produced as part of ESRC research into social identity and discrimination by Professor Alex Haslam, of the School of Psychology, University of Exeter.

Professor Haslam and Dr Michelle Ryan, also at Exeter, analysed reactions to previous research into women who have managed to break through the so-called 'glass ceiling' into company boardrooms. This had found that those women who do make it are more likely than men to find themselves on a 'glass cliff', meaning their positions are risky or precarious.

The 'glass cliff' research also showed that companies doing badly are more likely to appoint a woman to the board – but once performance picks up, other women are less likely to be made directors.

Today (6 September 2004) in a presentation at the British Academy Festival of Science, in Exeter, Professor Haslam says analysis of reactions to this earlier research found that what we perceive as scientific is clouded by our own viewpoints.

A survey on the BBC website found that women tended to believe in the 'glass cliff' effect. Men, however, were generally antagonistic to the notion, with one describing it as 'crap science', and another saying he was 'disgusted' by the research.

Professor Haslam says: 'We are more readily seduced by 'facts' that emerge as a product of 'science-like' science. And this is especially true if those facts bolster, rather than threaten, our sense of who we are and our place in the world.

'We should be particularly wary of those scientific "facts" that conform to stereotypes – not because they are less likely to be true, but rather because we are less likely to reject them as impostors when they are false.

'Perhaps too, we should be more open to science that does not reinforce prejudices, such as The Glass Cliff study. This is not because it is more likely to be true, but rather because we are more likely to reject it as false when it is not.'

According to the online survey, 17 per cent both of males and females believed women were more suited to dealing with a crisis and more willing to take risks.

Around 20 per cent of women believed that their sex was singled out for inferior positions in companies, whereas only four per cent of men held this view. And 18 per cent of the women thought that men in senior positions preferred to hire other men for 'cushy' jobs. None of the men surveyed took this view, however.

Seventeen per cent of women thought they were seen as more expendable than men, as compared with none of the men believing that.

Those women who do make it are more likely than men to find themselves on a 'glass cliff', meaning their positions are risky or precarious

Women have fewer opportunities than men and therefore accept riskier positions, according to 31 per cent of women, but just eight per cent of men. However, only three per cent of women thought that the women were not picked for precarious leadership positions, as compared with half of the men.

■ The above information is from the ESRC's website which can be found at www.esrc.ac.uk, or see page 41 for address details.

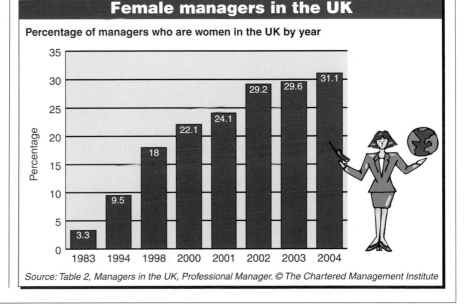

Female managers in the UK

Percentage of managers who are women in the UK by year

Year	Percentage
1983	3.3
1994	9.5
1998	18
2000	22.1
2001	24.1
2002	29.2
2003	29.6
2004	31.1

Source: Table 2, Managers in the UK, Professional Manager. © The Chartered Management Institute

Losing your job is 'worse than losing a loved one'

Unemployment scars can last a lifetime

Losing a job is more traumatic than divorce or widowhood, according to a study.

The unemployed are scarred for life even if they find a new job, researchers found.

One described unemployment as the 'social equivalent' of a car crash.

The destabilising effect can be so severe that many who experience unemployment cannot face working again.

But even those who return to the workforce never recover the levels of happiness or sense of well-being they had before.

That contrasts with those who go through divorce or widowhood, many of whom return to previous levels of happiness.

The findings contradict previous research which suggests that people return to a similar level of happiness after a positive or negative event.

The unemployed are scarred for life even if they find a new job, researchers found

---

The research was conducted by academics at Brunel University with economists and psychologists in the US and France.

Dr Yannis Georgellis, lecturer in labour economics at Brunel, said: 'The message from our research is clear. Losing your job, however briefly, scars you for life, causing much more long-term damage than divorce or widowhood.

'Our findings suggest that far from being an unfortunate by-product of economic change, unemployment could in itself have a serious destabilising effect on the future development of our labour markets.

By Darren Behar, Industry Correspondent

'There are thousands of highly-skilled workers out there who have lost their jobs, and as a result cannot face working again. Not only is this wasteful, it can also reduce countries' competitiveness.

'Our research shows that unemployment is the social equivalent of a car crash. Its psychological effects are severe and permanent. More worryingly, the longer the period of unemployment, the more severe these effects become.'

Meanwhile, redundancy rates for Britain are at record lows, with just six in 1,000 people being axed over the winter.

Unemployment has also reached a new low and more people are in work than at any time since 1984 when comparable records began, the Office for National Statistics revealed yesterday.

The unemployment figure fell by 48,000 in the three months to March to 1.41 million, the lowest total since 1984.

The number of people in work reached 28.35 million in March, a rise of 195,000 over the first three months of the year.

The numbers claiming unemployment benefit fell by 6,000 in April to 876,300, the best figure since August 1975.

The Prime Minister claimed the figures showed 'one more person in work every two minutes since this Government has been in power'.

But critics said they mask the continued collapse of manufacturing. Jobs in manufacturing firms fell 101,000 in the past year to 3.4 million, the lowest since those records began in 1978.

■ This article first appeared in the *Daily Mail*, 13 May 2004.

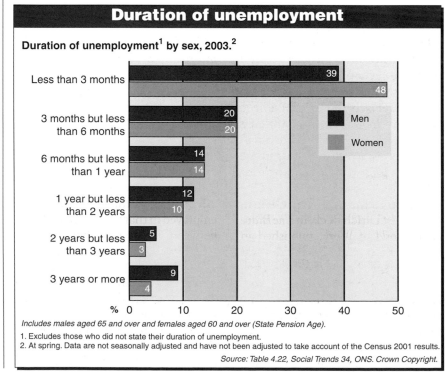

Duration of unemployment

Duration of unemployment[1] by sex, 2003.[2]

	Men	Women
Less than 3 months	39	48
3 months but less than 6 months	20	20
6 months but less than 1 year	14	14
1 year but less than 2 years	12	10
2 years but less than 3 years	5	3
3 years or more	9	4

% 0   10   20   30   40   50

Includes males aged 65 and over and females aged 60 and over (State Pension Age).
1. Excludes those who did not state their duration of unemployment.
2. At spring. Data are not seasonally adjusted and have not been adjusted to take account of the Census 2001 results.
Source: Table 4.22, Social Trends 34, ONS. Crown Copyright.

Work this way

You'll need to be flexible to get a job in 2020, but firms will also have to be flexible to keep you, says Liz Stuart

A trip forward in time to Head Office, 2020. You cannot even begin to think about the new skills required of you, the new methods of getting the day's graft done, because one thing keeps nagging at you: where are the desks? And where are the people who used to sit at those desks? There seems to be just a handful of people about, gathered in small groups. Some stand as they work on handheld computers, others sit in groups, on clusters of chairs. Even the office itself is tiny. The huge glass and chrome monstrosity the company put up in the 1980s has long since been sold off – with fewer people to accommodate, there will be no need for sprawling blocks.

Predicting the future of work is not a science. The vision above is that of Michael White of the Policy Studies Institute, the co-author of *Managing to Change*, which was published as part of the Future of Work research programme. Will his prediction be any more accurate than those of some of the illustrious names who have preceded him in foretelling the future?

John Maynard Keynes wrote in 1930, in *The Economic Possibilities for Our Grandchildren*, that by the end of the 20th century we would all be working just five hours a week. In 1996, Jeremy Rifkin soothsaid the end of work altogether. In the 21st century, he predicted, employment would be phased out, at least in the industrialised world. Jobs would be taken over by machines and workers forced on to the dole. The German sociologist Ulrich Beck, in *The Brave New World of Work*, published in 2000, claimed the work society was disappearing. The working environment of the future, he said, will resemble that of Brazil, with no permanent jobs, only informal and insecure labour.

Going by current trends, Keynes's proposition is impossible and Rifkin's

and Beck's seem implausible. So can we take a guess at how we will be working in 2020?

In 16 years' time, most employment in Britain will still be structured much as it is now: the majority of us will still be working for other people, mostly in a place other than our homes, doing a job instantly recognisable today. There probably will not have been a wholesale shift to an itinerant workforce. An example from the immediate past proves the need for caution when predicting change: the fastest-growing occupation in the 90s was not software engineering (although the numbers employed in that trade grew by 185% between 1992 and 1999) or even telephone sales or business consultancy (106% and 93% respectively). The real growth industry, at a massive 302%, was the distinctly low-tech job of hairdressing.

In the words of Richard Pearson, the director of the market research centre the Institute for Employment

Studies, rather than being about sweeping changes, the future is about 'evolution, rather than revolution'.

So how will we be working in 16 years' time? The answer, of course, is far from certain. Most of the government's peering into the future takes us only as far as 2010 – such as the work done by the Department of Work and Pensions, and the Department of Trade and Industry's Foresight team. As Alexandra Jones, a senior researcher at the Work Foundation, says, predictions past that date become 'a lot wobblier'.

But there is some evidence to provide us with ideas. From his base in Leeds, Professor Peter Nolan runs the Future of Work programme, a huge research project which has been running under the auspices of the Economic and Social Research Council for six years and across 22 UK universities. He paints a picture of a growing divergence between those employed in highly skilled, highly paid professions, and those at the bottom of the employment chain. The economy of work, he believes, will be increasingly hourglass-shaped.

'At the top end of the jobs hierarchy, people are likely to enjoy substantial discretion over their hours, places and patterns of working time. But this will be fuelled by the growth of low-paid and unskilled labour, doing jobs that would have been familiar 100 years ago,' says Nolan. He predicts managers and those in the professions will have job security. And, contrary to the predictions of futurologists, the majority of employees are likely to continue working for an organisation, rather than for themselves, or for a series of different people. In 2020 nine out of 10 jobs will still be permanent, although maybe not full time, he says.

Flexible working is the mantra of those who seek change in the way our working lives are structured – in the first six months of this year, this newspaper alone carried 67 stories that mentioned the phrase 'flexible working'. The government has given employees the right to request flexible working patterns, and last month's (August 2004) *Guardian*/ICM poll showed a strong appetite for greater flexibility, especially among young workers. That hunger is likely to have been satisfied by 2020, by which time the way our jobs are structured will have changed massively. Many people will work as employed freelancers. People will be trained to work on a wide range of different projects, liaising with experts outside the company when additional help is needed. Companies will be smaller and more specialised. Jones says management structures and hierarchies will flatten out, giving workers more control over their jobs.

Offices will be for 'face time' only, when meetings in the flesh are essential, says Jones. Everything that can be done from home, will be. That will have wider benefits, too. Half the greenhouse gas emissions in Europe are the result of office work – people's journeys to and from their workplace, and heating and air conditioning once they are there – according to figures from the European commission. While home-workers will still need to keep warm, there will be much less wasted energy use.

But our connections with our employers might actually become more profound, even if we spend less time with co-workers. We are likely to stay in our jobs for longer as we learn and develop within the company, and so become less likely to look for another job. Keeping staff is vitally important in the service sector, and Jones believes employers will finally have woken up to the paradox that to keep someone on, you need to keep developing in them precisely those skills that would equip them to leave and find a job elsewhere.

Companies that want to retain staff will also have to take a more relaxed attitude to time. Jones envisages careers being seen as a landscape, with peaks and valleys of working hours, allowing the young to work longer, those with families to work less, and retirement to be

phased in gradually. All workers, not just those with children, will be allowed to take time out to study or travel. Inevitably, that would require us to manage our own careers and finances, particularly securing our pension provision.

John Cridland, the deputy director general of the CBI, agrees. He thinks that by 2020 there will be no fixed hours, or job descriptions: everything will be up for negotiation. 'This will definitely be the case with managerial and professional jobs, but also in other service jobs too. Obviously you need staff in a restaurant at the same time as customers, but provided the basics are covered, there'll be no point in having lots of people with the same set of skills.'

Flexible working is the mantra of those who seek change in the way our working lives are structured

---

More jobs will be open to more people as well. White hopes that by 2020 every other person working would be a woman, particularly in senior roles, 'although I think it's unlikely to be 50-50 by then', he says. While gender parity will not yet be a reality, women in the 2020 workplace will be better able to realise their career aspirations. 'Put it this way, it's going to have to change because women are just not going to put up with things like glass ceilings in the future,' says Nolan.

That process will be aided by men playing a greater role in caring for their children and their parents: by 2021 there will be 12 million people over the age of 65, so the burden of care will have to be more evenly shared. Instead of men working 60 hours a week and women working 20, it is likely that many couples will opt to split the workload, as well as their responsibilities at home – so we could well see both partners choosing to work a 35-hour week, with the costs of additional care subsidised by the government. Care provision will be another area in which employers see the chance to build loyalty among

their staff. Workplace nurseries will be more common, and technology will boost parental confidence in them, with webcams allowing mothers and fathers to check on their children whenever they choose.

It will not only be women who secure higher status in the workplace. There are already a million disabled people who say they want to work, according to the Disability Rights Commission, and that figure will grow as the workforce ages – particularly as disability includes conditions such as diabetes and severe heart problems, as well as long-term depression. In the sardine-tight labour market of 2020, that will be a group employers will not be able to ignore.

Cridland feels more progress will also have been made towards racial integration in the workplace. 'For instance, many African-Caribbean male teenagers have a greater tendency to rebel and opt out of education when they are younger, although they go back into learning when they are older,' he says. 'Some employers are already realising they need to do more outreach work to get to these groups: in a tight labour market, and as service sector employers realise they need employees who reflect the communities where they work, they really need to attract them as employees.'

There may also be more Pakistani and Bangladeshi women at work by 2020. Those two groups are currently badly underrepresented in the workforce, but research from Manchester University suggests that more of these women, particularly those with qualifications, will want jobs.

Older people, too, will be more prevalent in the workplace. Jones says the likely retirement age by 2020 will be 70, and many future-watchers predict that will rise even further – not only to counter the pensions crisis, but also to release the pressure on the labour market.

Nolan, however, disputes the notion that older people would stay on at work out of choice. 'That's fine if you're a lawyer or company director where you can pick and choose your hours and projects,' he says, 'but if we're talking about someone who's been working in a factory for 40 years, do you really think that they'd want to carry on for another five?'

The real beneficiaries of the changing nature of the workplace will be those who have low levels of skills but can none the less master technology, predicts White. At the moment, the opportunities open to those people may be no more exciting than working in a call centre, but new technologies should open up other possibilities. Cridland agrees, adding that everyone will be better qualified (by 2010 there will be 2m fewer jobs that require only GCSEs, for example), so employees will be valued for their skills rather than just for turning up. If they cannot master technology, however, the least skilled will have to settle for supporting the freer lifestyles of the their better-paid peers. And many, reckons Richard Pearson of the IES, will be forced to take second jobs.

Outsourcing, the issue currently animating both the incumbent and the aspirational president in the US, will continue. Reservation agents, computer programmers, database managers, financial analysts – all those whose jobs depend, in part, on an ability to master repetitive tasks performed on a computer – will have been relocated abroad. 'Only the customer-facing jobs will be left,' says Cridland.

But, he points out, the lost jobs will be replaced with shiny new ones, more suitable to our developing economy. He points to the banking giant HSBC, which creates two jobs for every one it sends offshore.

The bottom line about work, of course, is that we do it for money. Those who do it for hard cash in the hand might not be happy about some of the changes ahead: identity cards and the decreasing use of cash will make back-pocket payments harder, in effect formalising the black economy. That will, however, be a positive for those people, mainly women, who work off the books not to avoid tax but because their employers want to avoid giving them full employment benefits. The minimum wage is also likely to increase, and childcare and housework are likely to attract tax breaks, meaning people can afford to pay their nanny and cleaner more.

Ian Hopkinson, the head of employment tax at KPMG, thinks salaries will consist of totally flexible remuneration packages: we will be able to choose between pay and a combination of benefits, such as buying days off. While this is already happening in some workplaces, it will be the norm by 2020. He adds that while there are still likely to be behemoth salaries paid to City executives, wages will be far more transparent. Sadly, he also thinks it unlikely that teachers or nurses will see radical increases in their relative salaries. 'These are likely to remain in the private sector and future governments aren't going to be able to afford to pay them huge amounts,' he says.

Public sector workers will still negotiate their pay collectively, through trade unions. But in the private sector, where only 18% of the workforce now carries a membership card, the unions will have been transformed into professional service organisations.

'This needn't just be about providing things like insurance,' says Cridland. 'The downside of negotiating individual contracts is that you're not protected by collective bargaining. Unions in the future are likely to step in to assist individual members to negotiate pay.'

The presence of more women in senior positions and in better-paid professions means the gender pay gap will narrow, but it will not disappear. 'For that to happen would require a major revaluation of the contribution of women at work. We'd have to see the political will for things to change,' says Alastair Hatchett, the head of pay services at Incomes Data Services.

The Work Foundation predicts there will be a major revaluation, however, in the measurement of work. Some method will be found to measure output – the number of books edited or meals served – rather than input, the number of hours spent at your desk, it says. Others, however, are more sceptical. Pearson says: 'Theoretically it's a good idea for output to be measured rather than input but in reality, for the majority of jobs, it just isn't possible to evaluate in an equitable and affordable way. You start getting into value judgements – how do you judge that the output of one person editing a book is better than that of another?'

Finally, to the most important question. Will we be happy in our jobs? Sadly, in spite of all the corporate attempts to woo us, and the chance to work from home a couple of days a week, it seems likely we will be as discontent as ever.

'People are being more intensely critical and demanding about everything. They expect more from their jobs. It could be harder for companies to make people satisfied: they'll do what they think necessary to make people committed and content, but I think they just won't be quick enough on the work-life balance issues,' predicts Michael White. It seems the technological advances pictured by Keynes may not bring us joy. Look on the bright side though: at least we'll be able to discuss our woes via video-imaging, rather than by standing around the water cooler.

Workers in 30s suffer most from work-life imbalance

Information from UNISON

Workers in their 30s are so stressed by long hours, pressure at work and juggling caring for children that they are desperate to leave their jobs.

Just 54% of those in this age group are happy with their work-life balance and a mere 17% are happy to work until they are 70 – the lowest numbers among all age groups contacted by researchers at a group called the Employers' Forum on Age (EFA), which campaigns on ageism at work. The over 60s turn out to be the happiest at work, with 93% satisfaction rates.

The new survey comes ahead of the TUC's 'Work your proper hours day' on 25 Feb 2005, which will mark how many UK workers work unpaid overtime – £23bn worth, in fact.

The TUC estimated that date is the average date when all this extra unpaid work ends and staff actually start earning their proper pay.

'Everyone knows we work the longest hours in Europe,' said TUC general secretary Brendan Barber. 'Too many workplaces are gripped by a long hours culture, where staff are expected to put in unpaid extra time week after week.

'We are not saying that we should all become clock-watchers, but it's about time we called time on bosses who think the longer something takes the better the job is done.'

The EFA research also backs up worries over women's equality at work, as it found that just 24% of women in their twenties hold management positions, compared to 37% of their male counterparts.

UNISON national officer Ross Hendry said that the growing body of research on work-life imbalance shows how important it is to consider how working time is organised.

'Our members are incredibly dedicated to the services they provide,' he said. 'But their commitment is often exploited by those who are focused on hitting targets and controlling costs. Good public services are provided by well-motivated, well-trained, fairly paid, enthusiastic staff – not employees who feel exploited, tired and de-motivated. We need employers to realise they have a duty of care over their staff as well as over service users, so that they meet the needs of employees through embracing, not opposing, work-life balance policies.'

The group commissioned focus groups, in-depth and telephone interviews among nearly 1700 employed people aged 16-70 and cross-referenced its findings with statistics from the national Labour Force Surveys 2003/04.

■ Information is from UNISON – see page 41 for contact details.

© UNISON 2005

The time and the place ...

Not all jobseekers treat salaries as the factor – some seek work-life balance. By Emma Lunn

Most graduates expect their first job to involve slaving away from nine to five in a busy office under the watchful eye of their boss. But some companies are waking up to the fact that allowing employees to work part of the time at home can help them recruit the best people.

Dan Hawes, co-founder of the Graduate Recruitment Bureau, says graduates expect a flexible working policy and want to create a good work-life balance. The option of working at home one or two days a week can help achieve that. 'It's not always salary at the top of the list of what graduates want. Time is the new money.' His view is backed up by the Work Foundation whose 2003 UK Graduate Careers Survey showed that graduates value flexibility more than pay when looking at prospective employers.

Many of the varied roles in the IT and internet sectors – such as design, programming and development – are ideal for home working, as they can be done remotely. Many on-the-road sales, marketing and account management roles effectively have home as their base.

Modern technology, such as mobiles, email and voice-over IP software, can make your home as well equipped for work as any office.

'Companies could miss out on someone really good by insisting they work nine-to-five in an office,' warns Hawes. 'And it could offer advantages to the employer by giving the employee the freedom to set their own conditions and working hours.' IBM is one company committed to creating a supportive flexible work environment – it allows employees flexibility and control over how, where and when their work gets done. It sees what employees do as more important than where it is done or how long it takes.

Shell also has a flexible working policy covering all employees. Its recruitment manager Erum Loan says it is something the company uses to attract quality people at all levels. 'It encourages people to join the company and gives them the freedom not to be tied down to a desk job and having to come in and leave at a certain time. It helps them mould their work according to their personal obligations.

'We give graduates the tools to work from home. A lot of graduates may want to study for a second degree or further their education and working at home helps them do this and prioritise their work. What we focus on is "are they delivering what they are required to deliver?" It's not about just putting in the hours in the office.' However, working at home is not for everyone.

Some people may miss the social aspects of office life while others will simply struggle to get out of bed. Hawes says: 'It's something they have to be clear about in themselves. You will also need to be very self-disciplined to work from home.'

Liz Hagger, e-guidance manager for Graduate Prospects, says new graduates often need further training and supervision and could benefit from an office environment. She warns that some companies will offer home working simply to save money. 'The cost of providing an office in central London is huge and if they can get away without providing that, they might offer home working.'

Although BT is one of the main supporters and facilitators of flexible working, it does not encourage graduates to work at home too early on in their careers. Head of graduate recruitment Jenny Adams says: 'It's one of BT's key selling points and comes up quite frequently at interviews. If people are in sales and out meeting clients it makes sense for them to work from home and the flexibility is very well received.'

Graduates approaching companies that offer an option to work at home should make sure they will get the necessary support that enables them to do so. Having someone at the end of the phone to help you if you do not understand something is just as important as having the latest in office equipment in your spare room.

Regular team meetings and training can help graduates feel they belong at the company.

Some companies are waking up to the fact that allowing employees to work part of the time at home can help them recruit the best people

---

Some employees, including IBM and BT, have a hot-desking facility where dedicated office space is available to flexible workers who can choose to come into the office if the isolation of home working becomes too much.

Robert Hayward, 25, from Berkshire, has worked for marketing consultancy Resonates since May. He works at home all the time except for occasional meetings with clients and his manager. 'They brought up working from home at the interview. It sounded quite good, especially not having to commute to London every day.

'Sometimes it's difficult to get motivated but I can get from my bed to my desk in under a minute and I feel privileged, so I don't give in to the temptation to stay in bed. Being alone is really the only bad point and that because you live at work you have to be strict with yourself.'

Lucy Davidson, 26, used to work from home when she joined an IBM graduate training scheme. But she found the isolation was too much and decided she was better suited to office-based work.

'I was travelling and doing project-based work and had a laptop and a mobile. It was good working flexibly so early in my career – but, after a while, I wanted my own desk and I got lonely as I didn't have people around to bounce ideas off. As a graduate it's quite difficult as you still need a lot of coaching and I didn't really feel like I belonged.'

Annabel Kilner, 23, works in marketing in London for market research firm Fresh Minds.

She started working from home one day a week within three or four months of starting work.

'Being a smaller company, I knew they would be more flexible than a big company. I said to my line manger that it would be useful to me to work from home and he was fine about it.

'It's good to get away from a busy office and work in a quiet zone, especially when I need to concentrate or am writing something. Home working is something I will definitely look for in future employers.'

© 2005 Guardian Unlimited

Attitudes to flexible working

The attitude of organisations towards flexible working

- Neither
- Discourages
- Encourages
- Don't know

5%
24%
47%
24%

Base: All full/part-time workers (1,193)

Source: This table is taken from Flexible Working Survey Report (2004), with the permission of the publisher, the Chartered Insititute of Personnel and Development, London.

Flexibility for parents

All parents with children under two should have the right to work flexibly

The Maternity Alliance today (26 April 2005) calls for an extension to flexible working rights for new parents. This would allow all parents of children under two the right to work flexibly. Currently parents only have the right to request flexible working – and their request can be refused by their employers.

This recommendation is just one of ten demands set out in the Maternity Alliance's Baby Manifesto to improve the lives of parents and babies in the UK.

The right to flexible working is crucial to supporting parental choice in looking after their children in the first two years of life. It allows mothers and fathers to maintain the parent-baby interaction that is so important to the healthy development of their babies. It also allows breastfeeding to continue, and eases a baby's transition into childcare, whether formal or informal.

Flexible working is particularly important for low-income mothers who often cannot afford to use their full entitlement to maternity leave. All women are entitled to 26 weeks' paid maternity leave, followed by a further 26 weeks' unpaid. However, this unpaid maternity leave is rarely an option for low-income women who cannot afford unpaid time off work.

Ruba Sivagnanam, Head of Policy, Information and Campaigns, said:

'The right to work flexibly in the first years of a baby's life would make a real difference to many families, giving them the choice to both work and care for their young babies. Currently, too many parents have their request to work flexibly refused or face demotion or worse still have to leave their jobs in order to take care of their children.

'At the moment real choices for parents with very young children are only available to those that can afford them. The first two years of a baby's life are critical for its development.

Helping parents to balance work and family life at this early stage will be good for parents and good for babies.'

■ The above information is reprinted with kind permission from the Maternity Alliance – visit their website which can be found at www.maternityalliance.org.uk or see page 41 for address details.

© *Maternity Alliance 2005*

Work-life balance in the British economy

Findings from the Department of Trade and Industry

■ Employees want work-life balance – nearly four-fifths of employees (78%) believe they should be able 'to balance their work and home lives' as they choose and 95% believe that 'people work best when they can balance their home and other aspects of their lives';

■ Employees believe employers should provide work-life balance – nearly six-tenths of employees (57%) disagree that 'it's not the employer's responsibility to help people' achieve this balance;

■ Childcare is a priority – 85% agreed that employers should make a special effort to accommodate parents with young or disabled children;

■ Employees take their working responsibilities seriously – 60% said that employees could expect to change their working patterns if it would disrupt the business. This is an increase from 53% on a similar study in 2000;

■ Availability of flexible working has increased – in the last three years the number of employers offering part-time workings has increased by 17%. Availability of reduced hours for a limited period has increased 21%; job share 9%; term-time working, compressed working and annualised hours 7% and flexitime 6%. Only the availability of home working hasn't increased;

■ Not all flexible working options are equally available – working part-time was most common (available to 67% of respondents). This was followed by reduced hours for a limited period (48%), job sharing (41%), term-time working (32%) and a compressed working week (30%);

■ The most popular flexible working options are often not the most widely available – the highest uptake was for flexitime (55%) and home working (54%) which were available to 48% and 20% of employees respectively;

■ Businesses that offer flexible working have better industrial relations – 85% of employees in businesses that offer four or more flexible working options described relationships between staff and managers as good or very good. This falls as the availability of flexible working falls – the figure is only 55% for businesses that don't offer flexible working. Furthermore, just 6% of employees in businesses that offer four or more flexible working options described relationships between staff and managers as poor or very poor. The figure for companies that don't offer flexible working was 17%.

■ The above is an extract from the summary of *The Second Work-life Balance Study*, which was carried out by MORI for the DTI. View the entire PDF on the DTI website at www.dti.gov.uk

© *Crown Copyright*

Part-time and flexible working

Key facts at a glance

Part-time is no crime – so why the penalty?

Part-time work

There are 7.4 million part-time workers in the UK (ONS, 2004a). 78% of all part-time workers are women. Britain has the second highest proportion of part-time workers in the EU (Haroarson and Romans, 2005).

Two-fifths of women in employment in Britain work part-time, compared with 11% of men (ONS, 2004b).

67% of women whose youngest child is aged 4 and under work part-time, 63% of women whose youngest child is 5-10 work part-time, compared with only 33% of women who have no dependent children who work part-time (EOC, 2004d).

The main trigger for working part-time is not the arrival of the first child, but the second (Francesconi and Gosling, University of Essex, 2005). A woman who had an additional child aged 0-4 is almost eight times more likely to work part-time.

Female part-timers are on average more likely to work in the distribution, hotel and catering industries, in the banking industry, in cleaning, in charitable services, and in school and in higher education. They are also more likely to be in relatively low-level occupations in these sectors.

Both male and female part-time workers receive 40% less training than their full-time counterparts (Francesconi and Gosling). The skills gap between part-time and full-time workers is growing (Olsen and Walby, 2004).

Women working part-time earn on average 40% less per hour than men working full-time – a percentage that has not changed in thirty years (ONS, 2004c).

Part-time work has a 'scarring effect' on earnings. The longer a person is in part-time work, the lower their wages are likely to be, even if they return to full-time work. Women who have spent just one year in part-time work, and then work full-time, can still expect to earn 10% less after 15 years than those who worked full-time for the same period (Francesconi and Gosling).

> ## 78% of all part-time workers are women. Britain has the second highest proportion of part-time workers in the EU

Flexible work

The right to request flexible working, introduced in April 2003, has had minimum adverse effects on business (CIPD (2003) and Working Families (March 2004)). However, there is no evidence yet that the right to request flexible working is opening up in more senior jobs. Indeed managerial employees are the most likely to be excluded from any arrangement (Woodland et al, 2003).

The awareness of the right to request flexible working is not as high as it needs to be to become effective (EOC, TUC). In a survey of over 900 parents of disabled children, Contact a Family found that nearly half thought the provisions only applied to women (Harrison and Shelly, 2004).

An EOC survey found that while 4 in 10 workers say their boss would respond positively if they asked for flexible working, another four are unsure and a sixth say their boss would certainly not respond positively (EOC flexible working survey of awareness).

Fathers

Men's caring roles are expanding, whilst their earning role is not decreasing to the same extent (O'Brien, 2005).

UK fathers work the longest average weekly hours in the EU – 46.9 (O'Brien and Shermilt, 2003).

Carers

Across England, Scotland and Wales there are 5.6 million people providing unpaid care for another adult – 3.2 million women and 2.3 million men. 18% of households contain a carer (ONS, 2004f & GroS, 2004).

38% of mothers, 11% of fathers and 18% of carers have either left a job or been unable to take a job because of difficulties of combining it with caring responsibilities (EOC, 2004c).

While the availability of flexible work is increasing (Stevens, Brown and Lee, 2004) it is still limited. The prevalence of part-time work is strongly influenced by cultural assumptions about women's sole responsibility for children, the unavailability of suitable childcare and by what jobs are on offer in the local labour market.

ICM Polling

ICM interviewed a random sample of 2031 adults aged 18+ by telephone between 5 and 9 January 2005. Interviews were conducted across the country and the results have been weighted to the profile of all adults. ICM is a member of the British Polling Council and abides by its rules. Further information is at www.icmresearch.co.uk

Flexible working

An extremely high 82% of respondents agreed that the right to request flexible working should be extended to all parents and carers. 93% of women aged 18-34 agreed, including 42% who strongly agreed.

74% of Conservative voters, 89% of Labour and 86% of Liberal Democrat voters agreed. 86% of those likely to change their vote agreed that the right to request flexible working should be extended to all parents and carers.

In addition, when asked whether carers should have the right to ask their employer to vary their working hours an overwhelming 93% of respondents agreed. 44% of women aged over 55 strongly agreed. 40% of those likely to change their vote strongly agreed.

Over 60% of people thought the right to request flexible working should be given to all employees.

Part-time workers

EOC/ICM survey findings indicate that people want part-timers to be given the same treatment as full-time workers.

There was considerable support for part-time workers overall with 90% of all respondents agreeing that those who work part-time are just as likely as full-time workers to be committed to their jobs. Nearly half of all women respondents, compared to one-third of men, strongly agreed with this statement.

Over 80% of women, compared to 60% of men, agree that part-time workers should have the same promotional opportunities. Nearly 40% of women strongly agreed. One-third of men disagreed.

Over 50% of women strongly agreed that part-time workers should receive the same hourly pay as full-time workers doing the same job. An extremely high 90% of all respondents agreed with this statement.

■ The above information is reprinted with permission from the Equal Opportunities Commission – see page 41 for contact details.

Flexible working can keep your absence rates healthy

Research finds flexible hours, homeworking and special leave can cut absence in the private and public sectors

Flexible working can reduce sickness absence, according to new research. Flexible hours, homeworking and special leave have helped to cut absence in both the private and public sectors, the report *In Sickness and in Health* has found.

Olivier Bouley, general manager at employee benefits firm Accor Services, which commissioned the report, said companies that were proactive in addressing the most common reasons for absence enjoyed better attendance rates. 'The key factors are stress and work-life balance. If you don't address these, then you don't address absence,' he said.

By Julie Griffiths

The survey, conducted by the charity Working Families, covered over 41,000 employees. It found that the average absence rate was 7.3 days per employee, compared to the CIPD's average of 9.1 days in its 2004 absence report. Forty-six per cent of firms found absence had fallen in the past year. The top three causes for absence were stress, caring responsibilities and managing other work-life issues.

Flexible working was the best incentive in managing absence, said 85 per cent, while 76 per cent found a return-to-work interview was the biggest disincentive.

Brendan Barber, TUC general secretary, said flexible working would help firms to tackle stress and absence by giving employees more control over their lives. 'Many jobs are very stressful. Business directors have pressured jobs, but have control over them and recognition for what they do.'

■ The above information is from *People Management*, the magazine of the Chartered Institute of Personnel and Development, on 5 May 2005, with permission. For more visit www.peoplemanagement.co.uk

Flexible working

Information from everywoman

A flexible working pattern can be the ideal solution to balancing the responsibilities of family and working life more effectively. It can give you time to care for your child while allowing you to concentrate on your job fully when you are at work. It can, if managed correctly, be a lifesaver for you, and make economic sense to your employer.

An increasing number of employers are now introducing a range of family-friendly policies that allow their employees to achieve this balance and enhance the quality of their lives and those of their families. Flexible working practices to look out for, or ask your employer about, include:

Part-time working

Anything below the standard working week. It might mean you can leave early enough to pick the children up from school. But watch out for the boss who wants you to cram a full-time job into part-time hours or pay!

Flexi-time

Where you can vary your hours but have a fixed core time and can take banked hours as flexi leave.

Job-sharing

Where a job is split between two individuals.

Term-time working

Allows you to be in a permanent full or part-time job while taking unpaid leave during agreed school holidays. Your pay may be averaged out over the year.

School hours working

Where you work during school hours only (lets you drop the kids off and pick them up).

Compressed hours

Where you work more hours each day, but fewer days of the week.

V-time (voluntary reduction in hours)

Born in the USA but now in the UK, V-time allows you to reduce your time at work by an agreed period.

When considering some form of flexible working it is worth spending some time in researching which type of flexible working would suit you best and to make sure that you put a good case to your employer.

Working from home

Where you can work from home all or part of the week. Research suggests that professional and clerical jobs are the most suitable for home working. Whilst it can be done with older children, don't expect to be able to work and look after a baby at the same time.

- The above information is from the everywoman website which can be found at www.everywoman.co.uk

© everywoman

What are working from home and teleworking?

Find out about the pros and cons of a new way of working. Are these options you could consider?

Generally speaking, teleworking is where some or all of the work you do for someone else is carried out in your home. Advances in technology have meant that many jobs that, up until now, were tied to office buildings, can just as easily (sometimes more easily) be undertaken by people working from their own home offices. British Telecom reckons that there are about two million people working at home and that more than a quarter of them are teleworkers.

by Clare Brennan

Although there's no official definition of 'teleworking', it's usually agreed that it means using modern technology to help you work from home.

No set patterns define the teleworking arrangement between employer and employees. Circumstances vary, depending on the nature of the job and the functions of the company. What is clear is that, if it is properly thought through, teleworking can benefit workers and employers alike, and even have a positive social effect.

Benefits for employers

- Savings on office space
- Improved productivity – some surveys suggest that people working from home are up to 30 per cent more efficient than their office-based colleagues
- Retaining trained staff who might have had to leave because of a

change in their circumstances, for example, if their partner had to move because of their job or if one of their family needs to be looked after for a period of time.

Benefits for employees

- Less time spent commuting, so less stress and more time available for other activities
- Possibility to arrange work to suit individual working patterns or life choices
- Flexibility to cope with sudden emergencies.

Social benefits

- Teleworking means fewer commuters, so fewer cars on the road, so less traffic and less pollution
- People who work from home are in a better position to join in with local activities and so help build community networks.

When BT offered its workers the chance to do at least some of their work from home not long ago, 3,500 people volunteered within a month. Other companies have experienced similar levels of interest including local councils such as Oxfordshire and banks such as NatWest.

But there can be drawbacks to teleworking:

Potential problems for employers

- Monitoring work flow
- Assessing progress of individuals within the company

Teleworking is where some or all of the work you do for someone else is carried out in your home

---

- Cost of providing and maintaining the equipment the employee needs at home.

Potential problems for employees

- Creating a suitable, distraction-free space at home
- Loss of camaraderie and stimulation of contact with other workers
- Learning how to manage time effectively by saying 'No' to interruptions.

Potential pitfalls can be avoided if employers and employees carefully consider what they want from a teleworking arrangement and how to set it up effectively. For example, many people spend one or more days in the office in the course of a working week. This gives both sides the opportunity to communicate, evaluate progress and spend some time socialising and developing working relationships.

A number of trade unions have negotiated working from home schemes with employers and have produced useful guidelines for their members. If you are a member it might be worth contacting your union because they will be able to advise you on complicated matters, such as health and safety. This is a complicated issue. If you are working from home as an employee, for example, then your company has to make sure that your home meets health and safety rules. This is not just a question of checking electricity supplies, it means making sure that desks and chairs are ergonomically efficient as well.

Both sides must consider what equipment will be necessary for home working and agree who is to provide what. If there are other people in your house, you should discuss the consequences of working from home with them. (You don't want to make such a big change in your working life only to discover that it causes stress at home that outweighs all the advantages of flexibility and of not commuting.)

Employers and home workers should also be aware of issues such as insurance. If a company supplies equipment, then it usually takes on the responsibility for insuring it – it is cheaper for a company to add a laptop computer to its general insurance police than for an individual to insure one privately. You should always let your own insurance company know that you have started to work from home – sometimes this might gain you a discount on your household insurance as burglars will less likely to break in during day time.

- Reproduced with the permission of iVillage Ltd. For more information visit www.ivillage.co.uk

Becoming a working parent

Information from Opportunity Links

Starting a new job or returning to a career when you are a parent can be an exciting and challenging time. Getting used to balancing the needs of your family and the demands of paid employment can take time. Having confidence in your childcare arrangements helps. And don't forget you will have acquired useful new skills by becoming a parent which could include: time management, budget management, negotiation skills and flexibility.

Balancing work and home

The Government is encouraging employers to offer a range of policies to help parents balance the demands of their job with bringing up children.

Employers who provide work-life balance arrangements to help their employees could gain from:

- more loyal staff who don't need to take unauthorised leave
- an increase in the number of staff who return to work after maternity leave
- experienced and skilled staff staying on after they have children
- good returns on investment in training staff
- high levels of staff productivity
- better public image.

So discuss your needs with your employer or trade union representative.

Childcare help for employees

Your employer could benefit from getting involved in childcare.

Your employer could:

- provide childcare information for you
- provide information about the Working and Child Tax Credits
- get involved in your local Early Years Development and Childcare Partnership to find out more about childcare plans in the area
- buy some childcare places in local childcare services
- start up childcare services in partnership with others

- provide Childcare Vouchers or childcare allowances to help you pay for childcare.

Taking time off work

Sometimes you may need to take time off to be with your children.

Maternity leave – all employees are entitled to 26 weeks' ordinary maternity leave regardless of length of service. Ordinary maternity leave is normally paid leave.

Getting used to balancing the needs of your family and the demands of paid employment can take time

---

Women who have completed 26 weeks' continuous service with their employer by the beginning of the 14th week before their EWC can take additional maternity leave. Additional maternity leave starts immediately after ordinary maternity leave and continues for a further 26 weeks.

Additional maternity leave is usually unpaid although a woman may have contractual rights to pay during her period of additional maternity leave.

Paternity leave – eligible employees can take up to two weeks' paid leave to care for their new baby and support the mother.

Parental leave – employees – both mothers and fathers – who have completed one year's service with their employers are entitled to 13 weeks' (unpaid) parental leave to care for their child. Parental leave can usually be taken up to five years from the date of birth or in cases of adoption five years from the date of placement (or the child's 18th birthday, if that is sooner).

Parents of disabled children are entitled to 18 weeks' parental leave (previously 13 weeks) up to the child's 18th birthday, providing they have the qualifying length of service.

All employees are also entitled to take a reasonable amount of (unpaid) time off work to deal with an emergency or unexpected situation involving a dependant.

Right to apply to work flexibly – eligible employees who are parents of children aged under six, or of disabled children aged under 18, have

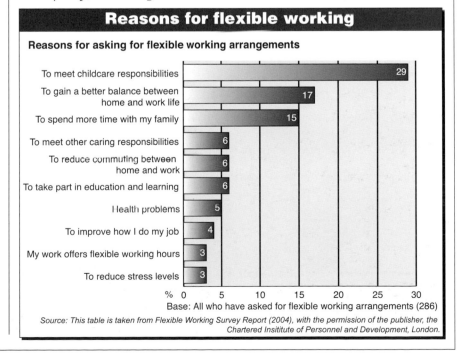

Reasons for flexible working

Reasons for asking for flexible working arrangements

Reason	%
To meet childcare responsibilities	29
To gain a better balance between home and work life	17
To spend more time with my family	15
To meet other caring responsibilities	6
To reduce commuting between home and work	6
To take part in education and learning	6
Health problems	5
To improve how I do my job	4
My work offers flexible working hours	3
To reduce stress levels	3

Base: All who have asked for flexible working arrangements (286)

Source: This table is taken from Flexible Working Survey Report (2004), with the permission of the publisher, the Chartered Insititute of Personnel and Development, London.

the right to apply to work flexibly. Their employers will have a duty to consider such requests seriously.

Flexible work

Sometimes you may need to fit your job around the demands of your family, especially while your children are young, when they are coping with new circumstances or if you have a child with disabilities or particular needs. Here are some options to discuss with your employer:

- working part-time or reduced hours
- job-sharing
- term-time working
- flexi-time – allowing you to choose your hours within set limits
- career break – unpaid time away from your job
- sabbatical – paid time away from your job
- teleworking – working from home.

Regulations that came into effect on 1 July 2000 remove discrimination against part-time workers and increase access to part-time work. This will mean better quality part-time jobs and more choice, which will help parents, women and men, to combine work with family life.

Arranging childcare at short notice

Every parent using childcare finds that there comes a time when emergency childcare could be needed. You could:

- build up a list of possible child-carers your child knows well – perhaps childminders who are friends with your childminder, for example

- reserve some annual leave for emergencies.

Further information on the Government's work-life balance campaign can be found at the URL www.dti.gov.uk/work-lifebalance

- The above information is reprinted with kind permission from Opportunity Links – please visit www.opportunity-links.org.uk for more information.

© Opportunity Links

Working from home

Achieving work-life balance while working from home

 W e all want to spend more time with our children. Is working from home the answer? Melissa Hill reviews the promises and perils of working from home.

Tele-commuting

Relying on your phone and computer to get your work done while you stay in your snuggly slippers can be a relaxed lifestyle. However, it is worth making sure that you can actually get work done with children playing at your feet. If not, you may still need full-time childcare. If your employer is willing, agree to work from home one day each week for a trial period so you can both establish at an early stage what problems, if any, there may be.

Freelance work

There are a variety of skills that companies outsource to freelancers, and it can be a fun and lucrative way to work. However, make sure you don't become dependent on a single company for workflow. Many small businesses have gone under because of an over-reliance on one big client for their contracts. Not only can income become unreliable. Drumming up new business is work-intensive and it can make you less available for your family.

Contract sales

There are a number of businesses that are dependent upon at-home mothers for selling their product through demonstration parties or catalogue distribution. The work demand is generally low, while the need for selling skills varies according to the company. For people with good social skills, this can be an enjoyable way of earning a bit of money. To avoid being taken advantage of, stay with brands and companies with which you are familiar. This will make both you and your customers feel confident and secure.

Starting a home business

One at-home mother who left the business she had founded commented that she would never start a business from scratch again. New businesses often require an overwhelming amount of loving attention. Test home business ideas gradually. If your priority is to spend more time with your family, find a business that can fit flexibly around the children's schedule. There is nothing wrong with slow growth in a home business. Avoid taking on investors at too early a stage. They may pressure you to grow profits at the expense of your other priorities.

- Melissa Hill, a writer and commentator on work-family balance issues, is the author of *The Smart Woman's Guide to Staying at Home* (Vermilion, paperback, £9.99) and an at-home mother of two. Half of her personal income from sales of *The Smart Woman's Guide* are pledged to the domestic abuse charity, The Women's Aid Federation of England.

The above information is from the website www.everywoman.co.uk

© Melissa Hill

Work and childcare

Childcare provision is not geared to realities of modern working life

For most of the growing number of women who go out to work, organising childcare for young children is a highly complicated process in which the slightest disruption is likely to cause a crisis, according to new research sponsored by the ESRC.

Among big city-dwellers, pre-school arrangements – even for the most affluent households – involve careful scheduling in time and travel, typically using three or four different types of regular care, says the study, led at University College, London, by Professor Linda McDowell.

For many families, jobs have become increasingly insecure, temporary or casual, and the hours demanded have either increased or become less regular in terms of day and night shifts and the working week, says the report.

The growing dominance of low-paid service sector work makes it increasingly difficult to have reasonable living standards from a single wage, so forcing many working-class couples to have two or more jobs in order to survive.

This study examined, among other things, who does what in the home when both partners are working. And

it investigated how childcare is arranged and managed if parents work shifts.

Focusing on younger families in two major centres – London and Manchester – the study found that while men are getting more involved in domestic tasks, in most cases it is still women who bear the brunt. And it is mostly women who sort out the details of how they and their children get to and from various workplaces, schools, social services, play areas and other often widely-spread sites.

Women are most often responsible for organising and scheduling domestic tasks, even among the more affluent, who can pay others to do things for them. But while women organised care whether they lived in London or Manchester, and regardless of their social class or neighbour-

hood, there were differences between and within the cities in the jobs people did and how they sorted out childcare. Single parents, for example, are less likely to be in waged work in London as the costs of childcare are prohibitive.

When it comes to working and finding someone to look after small children, the study says it is clear that current policies fail to take the complexity of the modern situation into account.

Professor McDowell said: 'We need to think about the ways in which different forms of care might be made more compatible and accessible, whether in terms of hours of provision, costs, or location in a neighbourhood.

'For many of those we interviewed, cost as well as quality is a key issue. High quality care is expensive, especially in London, and there are implications in this not only for individual parents but for those who offer a service.

'As other research has revealed, new nursery places are often short-lived as local parents cannot afford the high costs, especially when the quality of staff which most parents want tends to raise the price beyond their reach.'

More women in better-off households are going to work, mostly full-time, as higher and further education opens up new opportunities. But the study found a growing difference between their living standards and those of women at the other end of the scale. And this difference is becoming more polarised as the service sector expands. It is also clear that many women, in all social classes, have interrupted working lives, with longer-scale implications for their financial independence and later for their pension provision.

■ The above information is from the ESRC – visit www.esrc.ac.uk or see page 41 for contact details.

© ESRC 2005

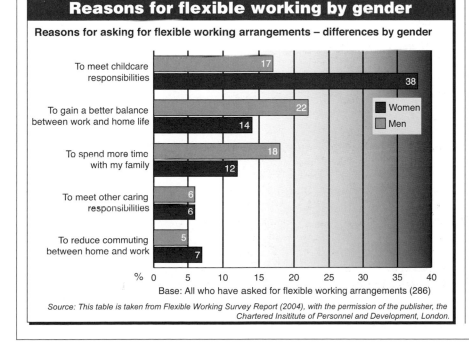

Reasons for flexible working by gender

Reasons for asking for flexible working arrangements – differences by gender

Reason	Women	Men
To meet childcare responsibilities	38	17
To gain a better balance between work and home life	14	22
To spend more time with my family	12	18
To meet other caring responsibilities	6	6
To reduce commuting between home and work	7	5

Base: All who have asked for flexible working arrangements (286)

Source: This table is taken from Flexible Working Survey Report (2004), with the permission of the publisher, the Chartered Insititute of Personnel and Development, London.

Facts about working dads

Information from Fathers Direct and the Equal Opportunities Commission

The EOC briefing 'Facts about Dads' brings together a short summary of statistics and research findings about fathers and employment, their changing role within the family and how changing expectations require new, more flexible approaches to working practices. The EOC wants to see caring roles shared, so that women and men share responsibility for work at home, and wider society and employers support people who look after their children or relatives and go out to work, making it possible to balance both and enjoy life. The EOC has commissioned several research reports into fathers and employment.

This briefing draws on the findings of two EOC research reports and other sources to present some of the key facts about fathers' employment patterns, their changing role within the family and how changing expectations require new, more flexible approaches to working practices.

Working long hours

Fathers are more likely to be employed, and to work longer hours, than men without dependant children.

- 4.6 million male employees in Great Britain have dependent children – over a third of all male employees.[1]

- 89% of fathers are in employment compared with 74% of men without dependent children.
- Fathers are less likely to work part-time (4%) than men without children (9%), unlike mothers, who are more likely to work part-time (60%) than women without children (32%).[1]
- UK fathers work the longest hours in Europe – an average 46.9 hours per week, compared with 45.5 hours in Portugal, 41.5 hours in Germany, 40 hours in France and 35.5 hours in France.[2]
- Around one in eight fathers in Great Britain work excessively long hours of 60 hours or more, and almost 40% of fathers work 48 hours or more a week.[2]
- While 80% of fathers and mothers are satisfied with their working hours, satisfaction levels drop to 60% for men working more than 48 hours a week and to 50% for those working more than 60 hours a week.[3]
- Fathers working more than 50 hours a week spend less time looking after children than fathers working shorter hours.[2]

Spending more time with children

Younger men's aspirations are different to previous generations.

- Fathers are spending more time with their children: in the late 1990s, fathers of children under 5 were spending an average two hours a day on child-related activities, compared to less than a quarter of an hour per day in the mid 1970s.[2]
- Fathers' time spent with their children accounts for one-third of total parental childcare time.[2]

Around one in eight fathers in Great Britain work excessively long hours of 60 hours or more, and almost 40% of fathers work 48 hours or more a week

---

- Where mothers work, one-third cite fathers as the main child carer while they are at work.[2]
- Some fathers sacrifice their own career ambitions in order to spend more time with their children at a certain point in their lives.[4]

'The value of the father as a child carer is vastly underrated. I do spend quite a lot of time with him, and I think I am equally capable as his mother at looking after him.' Father of 5-year-old child, working in the public sector.[5]

-I HAD A NIGHTMARE THAT I CAME HOME FROM WORK -AND YOU'D ALL GROWN UP!

...LIKE WHAT HAPPENED WITH YOUR DAD

Gender pay gap makes the problem worse

The fact that men's earnings are generally a higher proportion of the family income than women's can limit the time men are able to spend with their children. Different patterns emerge where women earn more.

- Women's hourly earnings from full-time work are 19% less than men in full-time work – and women's earnings from part-time work are 41% less than men's for full-time work.[1]
- Women's lower pay levels mean that it is women in the main who reduce working hours after children are born, reinforcing traditional gender roles in many families.
- Men are more closely involved in looking after children where the mother earns more than they do.[2]
- Women earn the same as, or more than their partner in a quarter of couples where both partners are working 16+ hours per week in 1996/97.[6]

Father-friendly employment

- Many employers still see flexible working or family-friendly working policies as something for women.
- Male-dominated workplaces, especially in traditional craft industries and occupations are less likely to offer flexible working arrangements than other employers.[4]
- Fathers often feel discouraged by workplace norms and culture from taking time off work for family, or expressing a wish for flexible work.[4]
- Fathers' expectations about whether they would have access to work-life balance policies are lower than for mothers.[2]

'I think it's probably tougher for fathers because the sort of impression you get is that women are the people who go and take the kids to the doctor's, they pick them up from school. The mothers have to be more flexible than the fathers in doing that. So there's more pressure for the father to stay in the job, stay there and keep on working.' Private sector, HR Manager.[5]

The lack of opportunity for fathers to use flexible work practices to look after children is worrying, as children whose fathers have been actively involved in their lives have better outcomes,[2] including:

- higher educational achievements

- more satisfactory relationships in adult life
- protection from mental health problems
- less likelihood of being in trouble with the police
- early involvement of father with child is associated with continuing involvement with that child through childhood and adolescence.[2]

The key thing that fathers request is flexibility and understanding from employers – even limited flexibility can allow many fathers to play a more active role with children such as attending sports days, having time off for family emergencies or for hospital appointments.[5]

Fathers often feel discouraged by workplace norms and culture from taking time off work for family

---

'... if I could have, even if it was one day a week, where I was out of here at 4pm to be home by 5pm, then I think that would be great.' Father of child aged one, employed in the private sector.[5]

References

1. EOC (2003) *Facts about women and men in Great Britain 2003.* Manchester: EOC
2. O'Brien,M & Shemilt,I (2003) *Working fathers: earning and caring.* Manchester: EOC
3. Worklife Balance Survey 2000 (as quoted in *Working Fathers: Earning and Caring,* see ref 2 above)
4. Dex, S (2003) *Families and work in the twenty-first century.* York: Joseph Rowntree Foundation
5. Hatter, W et al, (2002) *Dads on Dads: Needs and Expectations at Home and at Work.* Manchester: EOC
6. Pullinger, J & Summerfield, C (eds) (1998) *Social Focus on women and men.* London: The Stationery Office

- This information is from Fathers Direct, using information from the Equal Opportunities Commission – see page 41 for address details.

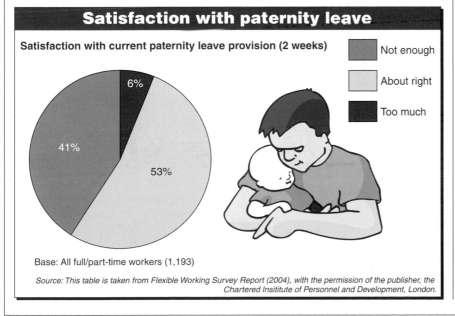

Satisfaction with paternity leave

Satisfaction with current paternity leave provision (2 weeks)

- Not enough
- About right
- Too much

6%
41%
53%

Base: All full/part-time workers (1,193)

Source: This table is taken from Flexible Working Survey Report (2004), with the permission of the publisher, the Chartered Insititute of Personnel and Development, London.

Mothers on the run

Despite more hours at work, there's always more to do at home

Dramatic changes in working patterns have taken place in the UK, particularly in the rise of women in employment. Three-quarters of households now have dual incomes, but women still take responsibility for most of the housework, according to research funded by the ESRC.

It is predominantly women who take time off to look after sick children, including 60% of women who earn the same or more than their partners

Despite institutional and legislative changes intended to reduce inequality and improve work-life balance, women are still finding themselves working long hours at home and at work and, for their trouble, generally receive less pay than their male equivalents. The project, carried out by Doctor Susan Harkness, Department of Economics, University of Bristol, studied the changes in female employment in the UK since the 1970s, a field that has seen little previous research. It focused on: working hours; times of work; income and wage premiums; and unpaid work such as housework and childcare.

As improved wage opportunities for women have emerged in recent decades, more and more married women have taken up paid employment. In 2002, 70% of working age women were in employment, a rise of 10% since 1979, and, over the same period, employment rates for mothers with pre-school children almost doubled. In contrast, the number of men in employment and the hours that they work has fallen.

'Despite recent progress, there remain employment inequalities between men and women. For example, less qualified women don't earn as much and are less likely to work full time than comparably qualified men,' said Susan Harkness.

'However, the pay gap is much narrower between men and women with degrees and there is some good news for less skilled women. They've seen the largest improvement in their relative labour market position, but it's still women who're doing most of the housework, regardless of qualifications.'

Despite men apparently working less, it is predominantly women who take time off to look after sick children, including 60% of women who earn the same or more than their partners. Working mothers with children put twice as many hours into housework as their partners despite the possibility of 'role reversal' in earnings. Housework is more evenly split in dual income households, especially when women earn as much or more than their partners and have no children. Of course, more affluent couples are able to afford to reduce their domestic burdens through hired help and by acquiring labour saving devices.

The pressures are really on for mothers working full time in dual earner couples and for single parents who work full time. Both long working hours, the burden of unpaid housework and childcare responsibilities have increased the time pressures for many women. The constraints that these pressures put on the energies of working women, particularly mothers, is seen to be holding back their earning power. Being on the run with work and family commitments provides little opportunity to concentrate on the actions necessary for career progression.

'Some of the newly introduced policies aimed at improving work-life balance, such as paternity leave, will help redress current imbalances,' said Susan Harkness. 'But others, like the new rights of full-time carers to request flexible working conditions, are likely, in my view, to reinforce current gender divisions in housework – because carers are usually women.'

Much has been said and written about work-life balance and this research adds further evidence for this debate. Some of Europe's longest hours at work for parents in full-time employment, and housework and childcare responsibilities taken on by working mothers has led to increased time pressures for many people. Breaking this cycle cannot be achieved by legislation alone and may require a complete cultural rethink.

■ The above information is from the Economic and Social Research Council – visit www.esrc.ac.uk, or see page 41 for address details.

© ESRC

Arranging a grown-up gap year

Taking a gap year from work is becoming more popular, but what's the best way to achieve it? What are the financial implications? And how can you make sure your job's still there when you come home? Gwladys Fouché tells all

There was a time when taking a year out was the preserve of school leavers and university graduates. Not any more.

More and more professionals are taking time out of the rat race, be it to help in the aftermath of the tsunami or admire the sunrise in the Sahara, by taking unpaid leave from their employers.

According to a recent YouGov poll of 2,000 employees, one in seven have already left the day job to go abroad, and more than 75% are thinking of doing the same.

If you're thinking of packing your bags yourself, bear in mind the following before knocking on your manager's door.

First, there is no legal requirement on firms to grant unpaid leave. It is a purely voluntary agreement between you and your employer, they are under no obligation to let you go.

However, the likelihood of them letting you take the time off is increasing. According to the Chartered Institute of Personnel and Development, 26% of companies now have a formal policy on career breaks, 16% have informal arrangements, and 4% are planning to introduce the scheme.

Why is it becoming popular? 'It keeps people long-term,' says Peri Thomas, human resources manager at Yorkshire Water, which has had an unpaid leave scheme in place for two years. 'It boosts staff morale and increases productivity. And it's good for recruiting new people.'

Yorkshire Water's scheme allows employees who have worked for the company for one year to take up to two years' unpaid leave. Many employees take time off to visit relatives abroad or do a full-time academic course.

Paul Edwards, a 29-year-old City banker, convinced his employers to let him take a four-month career break with the promise that he would return afterwards.

'I think they thought "if we say no, he might go" says Mr Edwards, who last year went to Bolivia to teach English before travelling on to Peru and Spain.

It also helped that Mr Edwards showed the possible benefits to his company. 'I said I wanted to learn Spanish and that going abroad would help me develop new skills after five years in the same job,' he says.

> *According to a recent YouGov poll of 2,000 employees, one in seven have already left the day job to go abroad*

Your employer is more likely to be sympathetic to your wishes if you, in turn, are sensitive to their concerns. Give them plenty of notice, say two or three months, and try to pick a time of year when business is quieter. Offer, too, to help arrange cover for your job.

'My boss's only concerns were about the practicalities of my leave: when I was going, for how long and who was going to replace me,' says Gillian Porter, 34, a married mother-of-one. Mrs Porter was the first person to ask for unpaid leave at the Manchester-based logistics company where she is a secretary.

But Mrs Porter, who volunteered in a Sri Lankan orphanage for nine weeks, is clear about why she was granted a break: 'If it had not been a humanitarian mission, I don't think my boss would have given it,' she says.

If your employer agrees to let you take time off, make sure you get it in writing. 'Specify the length of time you're going for, the return date, and check that your terms and conditions will not change,' says Nick Isles from the Work Foundation.

Think too about the financial implications, not just in the present but in the future. If you have an occupational pension, your employer's contributions may stop.

Staff at Barclays, which offers career breaks of up to 12 months for staff continuously employed for two years, will find that this is the case. However, British Airways, which has had an unpaid leave scheme for more than three years, continues to pay contributions to pensions, although only to people in managerial positions.

It may be worth considering what would happen if you needed to return to work sooner than planned, say because the money ran out or your plans fell through. A lot will depend on how your company covers your job while you are away.

At Yorkshire Water for instance, covering the job involves colleagues working overtime or employing temporary staff, so if a member of staff needs to cut their leave short, it is relatively straightforward to accept them back. If, on the other hand, another person has been seconded to your position, or contracted in, then things may be more complicated.

With careful planning and preparation, though, you should find yourself in the best position possible: on course for a life-changing experience, without the worry of quitting your job.

Working hard?

Manpower reveals why employees put in extra effort at work

Over 90% of British workers regularly put more effort into their job than is expected of them, and over two-thirds regularly do unpaid overtime. Leading employment specialist Manpower now reveals exactly why these workers go above and beyond the call of duty.

Surprisingly, we're not all in it for the money. Only 10% of the 1,113 people surveyed by Manpower selected financial reward as the reason they put in extra effort at work.

What gets the majority of us Brits going is the prospect of promotion. Over half (54%) of respondents highlighted career progression as the underlying motive behind working extra hard.

But it seems there are still people out there who are not so self-seeking. Over a third of employees (32%) cite their colleagues as the reason they put in additional effort in the workplace: many work hard in order to gain the respect of colleagues, while others feel a responsibility not to let their colleagues down.

The survey was carried out as part of Manpower's search for Britain's Most Valued Employee. Comments Charles Ashworth, Director at Manpower UK: 'In our quest to find the nation's most valued employee, we wanted to understand exactly what motivates the general public to work above the required level.'

Only 10% of the 1,113 people surveyed by Manpower selected financial reward as the reason they put in extra effort at work

---

'Whilst it's great to see that people are focused on their long-term career goals, what is really interesting is that over a third of people put in extra effort for the benefit of their colleagues and team mates. It is this type of employee – the employee who always goes the extra mile to make everyone's lives easier; who consistently performs above and beyond the call of duty and who is most valued by colleagues, that Manpower wants to celebrate as the nation's Unsung Hero.'

Manpower's Unsung Heroes competition – the search for Britain's Most Valued Employee is open to all companies and organisations whatever the size, and for all employees, both full time or part time, permanent or temporary. To enter, a line manager or employer must nominate their chosen employee(s) and provide examples of how each individual employee has made a difference to the business. The winner will win a fabulous all-inclusive seven-night holiday for two to Mexico, where they will get the once-in-a-lifetime opportunity to swim with dolphins.

■ The above information is reprinted with kind permission from Manpower – visit www.manpower.co.uk or see page 41 for address details.

© Manpower 2004

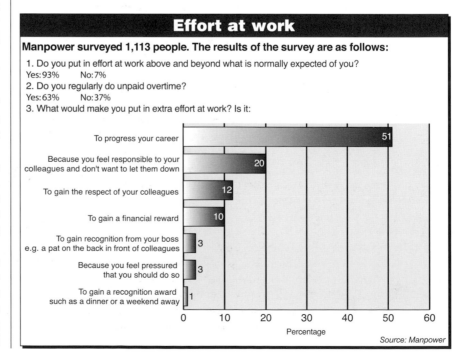

Effort at work

Manpower surveyed 1,113 people. The results of the survey are as follows:

1. Do you put in effort at work above and beyond what is normally expected of you?
Yes: 93%   No: 7%
2. Do you regularly do unpaid overtime?
Yes: 63%   No: 37%
3. What would make you put in extra effort at work? Is it:

Reason	Percentage
To progress your career	51
Because you feel responsible to your colleagues and don't want to let them down	20
To gain the respect of your colleagues	12
To gain a financial reward	10
To gain recognition from your boss e.g. a pat on the back in front of colleagues	3
Because you feel pressured that you should do so	3
To gain a recognition award such as a dinner or a weekend away	1

Source: Manpower

Are you a workaholic?

Does the sign in your office read 'I love Mondays'? Do you feel uncomfortable outside the orderly world of work? If so, you may be a classifiable workaholic!

Organising your work and your life

The truth is that it's just not possible to work ten or 12 hours a day, six days a week and still be effective. And anyway, achieving success in your career is not the same as having a fulfilling life. So, before you lose sight of your own needs, take a step back and look at what is happening.

Telltale signs

First you have to recognise the signs that you may be overworking:

- Do you feel that things won't get done properly unless you do them?
- Do you fear that you will be a failure if you don't work hard?
- Do you worry about the future, even when things are going well?
- Do you frequently work late at the office and/or take work home?
- Do you often work at weekends and at holiday time?
- Do you talk and think about work constantly – even when you are away from it?

*by Jane Smith
Careers Expert*

If you answered yes to any of the above, you have the makings of the next workaholism victim. So what can you do next?

Workaholism can creep up on you, and it can be just as destructive as drinking to excess

Some people work such long hours that they damage their relationships. Others lose their family, their home and their life. Tiredness and exhaustion can lead to mistakes, bad decisions, damage to property and personal injury.

The truth is that it's just not possible to work ten or 12 hours a day, six days a week and still be effective. The truth is that work-

aholism can creep up on you, and it can be just as destructive as drinking to excess.

Overcoming the problem

These days everyone has to work hard to get anywhere in their career – it's never an easy ride. The trick is to check that we are doing the right things in the right way and to maintain a healthy balance.

If you feel you are a workaholic, take a deep breath and resolve to change the way you live. Take some time out each day for yourself. Make sure that you do something exciting, relaxing or interesting in the evenings and at weekends. It could be taking some exercise, going to see a film, chilling out with friends, pursuing a new hobby. Whatever you decide, plan it well in advance, mark the time in red in your diary and recognise that these activities are important priorities in your life.

On top of all this, you must make sure that you stop for lunch and take other short breaks throughout the working day. Your aim should be to find a better quality of life and to rediscover some of the things that make the hard slog worthwhile.

- The above information is from the handbag.com website.

Young people at work

Thanks to Europe and action by the British government, rights for young people at work have just got better. This article explains how

Are you a young worker?

If you are aged 16 or 17 and in work then special rules about working time apply to you.

There are different rules for the minimum wage, which we explain later in this article.

Many other rights at work do not depend on your age. They are the same for everyone. You can find out about these on the TUC website www.worksmart.org.uk or in the TUC leaflet *Your Job and the Law* which you can get from the TUC Know Your Rights line 0870 600 4 882. This information only deals with rights that are different for young people.

Maximum working hours

There are rules to protect you against working too long each week and working at night. Normally you should not work:

- more than eight hours a day;
- more than 40 hours a week;
- or at night (but see below for more about night work).

But your employer can ask you to work longer hours if they are needed

for what the law calls 'maintaining continuity of service or production', or to respond to a surge in demand.

You can only do these extra hours if all these conditions are met:

- an adult is not available to perform the duties; and
- any training you are doing is not neglected or adversely affected; and
- you must be properly supervised if this work is at night.

Over-18s can agree to opt out of the 48-hour average weekly limit that applies to them by signing away these rights. Under-18s cannot do this. Even if you want to work longer hours, you cannot. Not every job is covered by this protection, though the list of exempted jobs is getting smaller. Members of the armed forces are not covered by these rules; and young seafarers are covered by a separate set of rules (the Seafarers Directive 2002).

Time off

You should get a proper break between stopping and starting work each day and a longer period off every week:

- you should get at least 12 hours of rest in every 24-hour period, and this should be a single 12-hour break;
- you should also get a rest period of at least 48 hours in every seven-day period – again this should be a single break.

This two-day rest day per week is twice as long as workers over-18s enjoy.

Again you cannot choose to give these up.

Meal breaks

You should get an uninterrupted break of 30 minutes if you are working for four and a half hours or more. You should be able to take this away from where you work.

Night work

Normally you should not work at night. For these purposes 'night' starts at 10pm and ends at 6am, though you can still be contracted to work past 10pm providing that you don't work between 11pm and 7pm.

There are some exceptions, however. Some young people will still be able to work at night, but only as long as the following conditions are met:

- the work is needed 'to maintain continuity of service or production' or to respond to a surge in demand;
- an adult is not available to perform the duties;
- your training is not adversely affected;
- you are properly supervised; and
- you are given compensatory rest.

If all of these conditions apply then you can work throughout the night if:

- you are working in a hospital or somewhere similar; or

Issues

www.independence.co.uk

30

- you are working in connection with cultural, artistic, sporting or advertising activities.

In addition you can work up until midnight or from 4am if you work in:
- agriculture;
- a shop;
- a hotel or catering business;
- restaurants and bars;
- a bakery; or
- postal or newspaper deliveries.

16- and 17-year-olds have a minimum wage of £3 per hour. The minimum wage for 18- to 21-year-olds is £4.10

The minimum wage

The age limits are different for the minimum wage.

From 1 October 2004 16- and 17-year-olds have a minimum wage of £3 per hour.

The minimum wage for 18- to 21-year-olds is £4.10 per hour.

The 'adult' minimum wage of £4.85 is only paid to those who are 22 or over.

Safety at work

The law says that employers must be extra careful with young workers.

Before taking on a young worker, employers have to assess the risks to your health and the suitability of the proposed work. They should take into account your relative lack of experience in the workplace.

There's a special TUC leaflet about health and safety for young people called *Work Safe* that you can get from the TUC Know Your Rights line 0870 600 4 882.

Unions today – your friend at work

At all times we need advice or support in connection with employment.

Everyone has the right to join a union – it costs less than you think and your employer doesn't need to know you are thinking of joining up. The average cost of being in a union is only 92p a week for part-timers and £1.99 for those working full-time.

To find out more about how to join a union and which union is the right one for you, phone the TUC's Know Your Rights line on 0870 600 4 882 or visit www.worksmart.org.uk/unionfinder

- The above information is from the TUC website which can be found at www.tuc.org.uk

The skills gap

Understand the current job market, then make it work to your advantage. With skills you're always welcome. Find out how to fine-tune yours

The biggest headache facing British industry today is an acute shortage of skilled workers. The UK currently has a million people unemployed, with a further 7.6 million people of working age inactive in the labour market, and yet, there remain over a million jobs unfilled. Many are asking, how did we get here?

Skills shortages are being experienced across the board, not just within the traditional problem areas of nursing and teaching. Accountancy, social work, medicine and, ironically, recruitment are all being severely affected. According to a recent survey by recruitment specialist, Reed, two-thirds of British firms are experiencing the crisis. The most desperate shortages of staff relate to specialist skills with 20% of employers complaining that they had problems filling posts requiring technical and engineering skills, 19% with IT and 16% with accounting skills.

by Dolly Dhingra

Employment minister Tessa Jowell said, 'A particular challenge for the future will be in IT skills shortages. We already know that over 18 million UK workers now require basic IT competence to do their job. There are 1.2 million currently employed at technician level, expected to grow by 20-25% in the next three years.' So bad is the lack of IT skills in Britain that a door-knocking campaign has begun to recruit set targets onto the government's Independent Learning Accounts, where online desktop computing skills are being offered at a bargain price of £25. 'Some commentators have estimated that, if we do not do anything to address this skills gap, 12 per cent of vacancies for professional IT jobs could go unfilled in 2002,' said Jowell.

Lloyds TSB periodic survey, Business in Britain, recently high-lighted the skills shortage within companies using their banking services. Managing Director Michael Riding says, 'The yawning skills gap is turning into a hazardous abyss across all sectors. In terms of recruiting unskilled staff, similar trends are also emerging.' Production line workers, shelf packers and internal postal workers – jobs that almost anyone can do – continue to remain vacant.

The UK currently has a million people unemployed, with a further 7.6 million people of working age inactive

---

But how has this acute problem arisen, and how did we fail to nip it in the bud?

The answers are not simple; there are several contributing factors.

Kevin Hogarth of chartered accountants, Ernst and Young, believes that the problem has been brewing for over a decade. Companies neglected to invest in training and recruitment, once the British economy moved out of recession and, by the 1990s, into a period of full employment (as defined by the late economist J. M. Keynes). An increase in young people continuing into higher education means that jobs that were previously filled by school leavers remain vacant. And when it comes to IT, few could have ever predicted the huge growth in new media jobs.

So, as things stand, the skilled worker is supreme, which is great news if you happen to be one. 'It's definitely a workers' market,' says Sarah Parsons of Reed.

The rise in demand for workers and the growth of the Internet has increased the speed and ease in which jobs can be advertised and applied for. Workers are moving from one job to another, far quicker than ever before, which means they are staying in them for shorter periods.

Andy Westwood of the Industrial Society offers anyone who is currently re-entering the workplace, or looking to change careers, the following advice, 'Make sure you visit your local employment services to get an overview of what jobs and opportunities are out there. What used to be a dead end visit to the job centre has now hugely improved. Personal advisers are able to help in all sorts of matters, from minimum wage issues to family credit. One-third of all job vacancies are carried by the employment service, so ignore them at your own peril,' he says.

Get in on the action

So what exactly is currently out there? Learndirect on 0800 100 900 is staffed by qualified career advisers and is open 9am-9pm Monday to Friday and 9am to midday on Saturdays. They can help with information on any educational course and course provider in the country. The country's largest database, Learndirect has information on over 500,000 courses. Over 75% of courses are available through the Internet. This is currently the largest e-learning network in the UK,

which means once you've registered, you can learn wherever there's a computer.

As things stand, the skilled worker is supreme, which is great news if you happen to be one

---

Highlighting just how huge the information generation has become, 400 courses alone cover the subject of information at Learndirect, from communication technology to designing your own web pages. For those wanting to work in small businesses there are courses on dealing with angry customers, understanding accounts and team-building exercises. Learning is vital to the UK's workforce, where over 7 million adults currently have difficulty with reading. 'What a lot of us fail to realise is that most of these people would struggle looking up a plumber in the *Yellow Pages* – they can't do the simple things that we often take for granted,' says a spokesperson for Learndirect.

There are 900 learning centres across the country, usually in accessible locations, such as shopping malls, schools and local community centres, which allow you to study en route to collecting the kids from school, or even after some shopping. Learning can now be adapted to your own personal timetable.

Underpinning this is the Independent Learning Account, a government initiative aimed at local skill shortages.

Eligibility is open to the self-employed, and those who wish to renew and refresh skills. Publicity for the scheme has been weak and the government is currently trying to meet large enrolment targets. Applicants to the scheme are being offered discounts of up to 80% on key courses. Childcare and travel costs are also on offer. Further information can be obtained by calling 0800 072 5678.

For mature women, the workplace has never been so good; an increase in recruitment agencies specialising in the older worker indicates that, employers are no longer shying away from the issue of age. Wrinklies Direct, a recruitment agency specialising in jobs for 'men and women of advancing years', now have 12 branches across the country. Candidates who are up on IT skills are almost guaranteed a position. Women over the age of 45 are particularly sought after, since they are unlikely to take maternity leave.

If choice was ever a misery for workers, it certainly isn't now when it comes to reskilling the workforce for the 21st century.

■ Reproduced with the permission of iVillage Ltd. For more information please visit their website at the following address: www.ivillage.co.uk

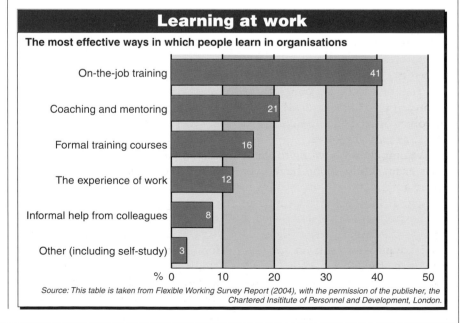

Learning at work

The most effective ways in which people learn in organisations

Learning method	%
On-the-job training	41
Coaching and mentoring	21
Formal training courses	16
The experience of work	12
Informal help from colleagues	8
Other (including self-study)	3

Source: This table is taken from Flexible Working Survey Report (2004), with the permission of the publisher, the Chartered Institute of Personnel and Development, London.

Skills shortage 12-year high

Over half of firms report recruitment problems

The UK skills shortage is at a 12-year peak, according to the Business in Britain survey from Lloyds TSB Corporate. Over half (52 per cent) of British companies experienced sustained difficulty in recruiting skilled staff in the last year – the highest level over the 13-year life of the survey. In addition, over a quarter of firms (28 per cent) reported problems finding unskilled staff.

Regionally, the East Midlands faces the biggest challenge, with 62 per cent of companies in the area experiencing a shortage of skilled candidates for jobs. Even London, with its considerable opportunities for the talent pool, fell below the national average with 46 per cent of respondent firms saying skilled staff were hard to find. Across the sectors, finding talented employees is a problem for 60 per cent of businesses in retail, transport and communications, and construction – the highest figures across all industries.

In addition, despite 49 per cent of businesses anticipating an increase in turnover over the first half of 2005, only 25 per cent expect to take on more staff – a drop on last summer's figure when 28 per cent of firms expected to increase their employee numbers.

Indicative of its slow growth as a sector, only 20 per cent of manufacturing companies are optimistic about taking on more staff this year. This finding supports figures published recently by the Office for National Statistics showing a fall to 3.24 million employees in the sector in the three months to January 2005, a drop of 92,000 on the previous year with over one million posts having disappeared since 1997.

Staffing is lower on the investment agenda than equipment and machinery for many companies, with 27 per cent expecting to increase their capital investment, compared with 25 per cent looking to raise their employment levels over the first half of 2005.

Peter Navin, banking director at Lloyds TSB Corporate, commented: 'A skilled workforce is integral to business success. Tax breaks and a favourable economic climate are only part of the picture. Because of the tight labour market, finding the right person for the job remains a challenge.

'Thanks to its general stability, Britain remains an attractive and profitable place to do business, but we need to ensure our workforce can compete globally, in terms of its level of expertise. Traditional employment pulls such as wages and benefits packages help maintain a competitive edge. By continuing to invest in management, training and resources, we can wage the war for talent with confidence.'

■ Information from Lloyds TSB – see www.lloydstsb.com

© Lloyds TSB 2005

Job crisis for school leavers

Rising numbers of top-grade students pose recruitment challenge for employers and school leavers

Rising numbers of students achieving top exam grades pose challenges for employers and school leavers alike, according to the Chartered Institute of Personnel and Development, the professional body for all those involved in the management and development of people.

Arguing that it is wrong to think that exam results alone have ever been a perfect way for employers to select the right person for the job, and for a more rigorous approach from employers to defining their requirements from job applicants, Rebecca Clake, CIPD Organisation and Resourcing Adviser, said: 'No one would wish to knock success. The results achieved by students in recent years are a credit to them. GCSE and A-level exam results remain a good indicator of basic aptitude.

'However, as employers find increasing numbers of students achieving the highest grades in exams, they are being forced to think carefully about how they differentiate between candidates.

'Our research shows that the main reasons for difficulties recruiting are a lack of suitably skilled and experienced candidates. It is, therefore, more important than ever for employers to set very clear job specifications that highlight what they really need. Exam results alone have never done this, and cannot hope to do so.

'Candidates too need to be giving more thought to how they present themselves in job applications. They should be aiming to emphasise why they are the right person for the job, by focusing on relevant work experience, extra-curricular interests and their commitment and enthusiasm for the post. This will be more effective than just relying on their exam results to tell the story for them.'

■ Reprinted with permission from the Chartered Institute of Personnel and Development – see page 41 for contact details.

© CIPD 2004

Business welcomes education white paper

Basic skills must be at the heart of education system, says CBI

The following information is reproduced from a CBI press release dated 23 February 2005. It is reproduced with the permission of CBI.

The CBI said today (Wednesday) that basic skills must be at the heart of the UK's education system and called for an end to pupils leaving school unable to read, write and add up.

The business community regards poor literacy and numeracy levels as the current education system's greatest failing.

Today's education white paper responds to last October's Tomlinson report, which proposed a major shake-up of UK qualifications. But the CBI has not been convinced by calls for radical reform.

Director-General Sir Digby Jones said: 'I'm delighted that A-levels and GCSEs are here to stay. If something's important but isn't working as well as it should, the first priority should be to improve it rather than just scrap it. This is what the government has decided to do with existing qualifications and I applaud them for it.

'Firms know and understand A-levels and GCSEs and are more concerned with what qualifications offer pupils than what they are called.

Business wants higher standards, not dramatically different structures.

'Proposals for radical qualification reform threatened to divert resources, attention and political will from tackling poor basic skills.'

47 per cent of employers are unhappy with young people's basic skills

The CBI has lobbied hard on education for over a year, urging ministers to concentrate on improving pupils' literacy and numeracy. New Education Secretary Ruth Kelly has responded to business concerns, saying no pupil should leave school without the sound grasp of literacy and numeracy that employers need.

Sir Digby said: 'Basic skills must form the bedrock of the UK's education system. Nothing can be more important for our country than bringing an end to young people leaving school unable to read, write and add up. I want to see the government both setting and meeting ambitious targets on skills. Let's get the basics right and also stretch the brightest pupils so that they achieve their full potential.'

CBI research shows that 47 per cent of employers are unhappy with young people's basic skills and a third are forced to offer remedial training to compensate for the failures of state education.

Business supports fully the vocational education objectives of the white paper. The CBI leader makes clear that business wants high quality vocational qualifications and is keen to work constructively with the government and schools.

Sir Digby said: 'Employers have been urging governments for years to prioritise vocational training so young people, parents and teachers do not feel their efforts in this direction are inferior to Higher Education initiatives. It must be crystal clear that young people have not failed if they leave education without a degree; they have failed if they leave without a skill.'

The CBI is calling for a national infrastructure for work experience to be in place by September 2006 to give pupils a sound knowledge and understanding of the world of work. The government should coordinate this and provide guidance so that work placements provide a worthwhile experience for young people and companies.

■ Please visit CBI's website at www.cbi.org.uk for more information or see page 41 for address details.

© CBI 2005

Qualifications

Population of working age:[1] by highest qualification, spring 2003

Qualification	%
Degree or equivalent	16.3
Higher education qualifications[2]	8.5
GCE, A-Level or equivalent[3]	24.1
GCSE grades A*-C or equivalent	21.7
Other qualifications	13.7
No qualifications	15

% 0   5   10   15   20   25

1 Males aged 16 to 64 and females aged 16 to 59
2 Below degree level
3 Includes recognised trade apprenticeship.

Source: Table 4.14, Regional Trends 38, ONS. Crown Copyright.

Is it really worth it?

Barbara Oaff asks final-year students and graduates if they think their degree will be money well spent in the long run

One day the headlines suggest graduates face gloriously sunny career prospects, the next utter gloom. So, just what is the truth? And what does it mean for you? Certainly, research indicates that vacancies are once again rising. After falling in 2002 and 2003 they rose 15.5% last year and are expected to rise a further 14.5% this year.

That's according to the Association of Graduate Recruiters, whose chief executive, Carl Gilleard, says the findings 'should bring a smile to the faces of those looking to enter graduate level employment'.

But many final-year students are not so convinced. A survey released just last month by the research company High Fliers reveals that almost two-thirds feel there are 'not enough graduate jobs for everyone leaving university this summer'. And their fears may be well founded. According to the Higher Education Statistics Agency almost four in ten graduates initially go into non-graduate jobs.

Of those who do secure a 'proper' position some will discover it is not their first big break after all. Benjamin Scott, co-author of *Turn Your Degree into a Career*, says: 'A significant minority of so-called graduate jobs aren't. They turn out to be nothing more than administrative roles – photocopying, filing, faxing, and yes, making the tea. There is no freedom to maximise your potential.' And Benjamin knows just how this feels. 'This happened to me and it was just so frustrating and so disappointing, especially after three years of hard work.'

A significant minority of so-called graduate jobs aren't. They turn out to be nothing more than administrative roles – photocopying, filing, faxing, making the tea

---

But hey, at least the money will be good, right? Well, yes. And no. The median starting salary is expected to hit £22,000 this year, a rise of almost five per cent on last year, the largest since 2000. And there's no doubting that those with a degree can earn above and beyond those without. The latest report from the Department for Education and Skills calculates that graduates eventually get an average of £15 an hour, A-level holders £10.50, GCSE holders £9.40 and unqualified school leavers £7.65.

But while the differential between graduate and non-graduate income is substantial, it is shrinking. In 2001 the Department for Education and Skills stated that graduates took home 51% extra than non-graduates. In recent years that has been downgraded; it now stands at 43%.

In either case, averages can be misleading. There is, of course, a band of graduates who will be paid far more than £22,000 – those who go in the City, for example, will typically start on £40,000 – and a band who will be paid far less. Twenty-seven-year-old Louise Horne, who has a first-class degree with distinction, speaks for a significant number of graduates when she points out that, 'five years after leaving university I have never earned more than £15,500 and am in the position many people my age find themselves in – I now have debt, no pension and no way of buying a house in the near future'.

To find out more about what graduates and graduates-to-be think about salaries, we asked graduate website Milkround.com to do an online poll. Perhaps not surprisingly, virtually none of the respondents thought salaries were too high. Around 57% said they were too low; 43% about right. However, over 60% were concerned about their own salary prospects.

Hannah Essex, education vice-president of the National Union of Students, is sympathetic to the mixed reality facing graduates. But she points out that 'a degree is not just about vocations. It is also about new experiences, new people, changing your attitudes, opening up your options.' Hannah admits it's a very expensive way to get your horizons broadened – but she feels that, 'for most graduates, having a degree does pay off, in one way or another'.

Investment analysis

Christopher Mairs is reading mathematics at the University of St Andrews.

'When I start I will be on £35,000 plus bonuses and benefits. I know that sounds like a lot but I also know I will be putting in long and pressured hours to earn it,' says Christopher Mairs, who could be described as one of Britain's elite graduates. This summer he will graduate from St Andrews – where he is the president of the university's Global Investment Group – and then, in November, start as an analyst for an investment bank in London. 'I do see myself as one of the lucky few, but I have worked really, really hard to make that happen.'

Teaching

Jenny Waller is completing a PGCE at the University of East Anglia.

Jenny Waller represents the position many graduates find themselves in. 'It's incredibly difficult to get a job – everyone thinks there's loads out there, but that's a myth. And even if you get one, it's not exactly big bucks.' Jenny, while really looking forward to being a teacher, knows the reality of getting in and on in the profession. 'It will be a lot of work and I will never earn a huge amount, but for me it's the best career ever and I wouldn't swap it for anything.'

Journalism

Veronica Browne (not her real name) read law at the LSE.

For someone who finds herself, like a significant minority of graduates, with a high debt and a low income, Veronica Browne, 23, is remarkably upbeat. 'I have a brilliant job, in a great company near Manchester. I'm on an appallingly low salary, but in this industry it's expected. And if you're not prepared to work for the going rate, there's a line of people behind you who will.' Veronica, who owes £18,500 and earns just £13,500, is a reporter on a design magazine. 'I could have chosen differently and earned a lot more, but I knew this career would give me real satisfaction, if not a real salary.'

© Guardian Newspapers Limited 2005

Modern Apprenticeships

An overview

What are they?

A real job with real pay while you continue learning. If you have not made a decision yet about which direction you should take after leaving school or college, Modern Apprenticeships are an option to seriously consider. We will not make a decision for you but will help guide and advise you as you move into the world of work. We will encourage you to make the most of your chosen route forward and provide you with an opportunity to work and continue studying for qualifications that you will need for a successful future.

What will a Modern Apprenticeship lead to?

- Employment with training
- A National Vocational Qualification (NVQ) at level 2 or 3
- Key skills, relevant to today's businesses, e.g. numeracy, communication, IT and teamwork
- Additional opportunities which could be technical, supervisory or professional
- Opens the door and leads directly to higher education including degree level.

Whether you started with GCSEs, GNVQs or A Levels, we will match a course to your needs.

Quality of training is regulated and monitored by the Learning and Skills Council, Awarding Bodies such as City & Guilds and meets exacting standards of the Adult Learning Inspectorate.

Who is eligible?

- Primarily those aged 16 to 24
- Not in full-time education
- Have ambition and motivation for success.

Grants to support Modern Apprenticeship opportunities are available for 16- to 24-year-olds or available at substantial discounts for those outside of this age group.

What can CWT offer?

- Employment from day one
- An individually designed learning plan
- Guidance from quality assured training advisers
- Commitment to support you until the apprenticeship is completed.

■ The above information is from CWT's website which can be found at www.cwtcov.co.uk

© CWT

Youth unemployment at all-time high

Youth unemployment is 'an economic waste', says the new ILO report

Half the world's unemployed are under 24, according to a new ILO study that charts the skyrocketing of youth unemployment over the past decade. Global Employment Trends for Youth, 2004 (Note 1) puts the global youth unemployment rate at 14.4 per cent in 2003, a 26.8 per cent increase in the total number of unemployed young people over the past decade. Although young people represent 25 per cent of the working age population, they make up as much as 47 per cent of the 186 million people out of work worldwide in 2003. Some 88 million young people, aged 15 to 24, are out of work.

GENEVA – Cutting the current youth unemployment rate in half would add some US$1.4 trillion, or four per cent of the 2003 global GDP value. Massive youth unemployment, the report warns, is also a social menace, breeding vulnerability and feelings of exclusion and worthlessness which may lead to 'personally and socially destructive' activities.

'Unless the potential of young people can be used in a productive way, neither they nor economies as a whole will face a bright future,' says

ILO Director-General Juan Somavia. 'Clearly, finding decent work for young people to staunch the youth employment crisis is one of the most significant challenges of our time.'

Global employment trends for youth, 2004 has found that rising worldwide unemployment hits young people – especially young women – hard. Those who do find work face long hours, short-term or informal contracts, low pay and little or no social protection, such as social security or other social benefits. One-fourth of the world's 550 million working poor

are young, meaning some 130 million young people are not able to lift themselves and their families above the US$1 a day poverty line. The majority of these young working poor are women, the report says. Young people are, thus, increasingly dependent on their families, and more and more susceptible to exploitation of any kind.

Youth unemployment rates in 2003 were highest in the Middle East and North Africa (25.6 per cent) and sub-Saharan Africa (21 per cent), and lowest in East Asia (7 per cent) and the industrialised economies (13.4 per cent). The industrialised world was the only region where youth unemployment saw a notable decrease (from 15.4 per cent in 1993, to 13.4 per cent in 2003).

The report shows that the growth in the young population is rapidly outstripping the ability of economies to provide them with jobs. It says the overall youth population grew by 10.5 per cent over the last 10 years to over 1.1 billion in 2003, while youth employment grew by only 0.2 per cent to around 526 million young people with jobs. Compared to the previous decade, youth employment-to-population ratios decreased in 2003 in all regions except the Middle East and North Africa, and sub-Saharan Africa. Less than one in every two young people who could work was employed in 2003, compared to slightly more than one in two people in 1993.

Young people have more difficulty finding work than their adult counterparts, the report says, with the global youth unemployment rate in 2003 at 3.5 times the global adult rate. While there is a correlation in most countries between trends in youth and adult unemployment rates, the report notes that during reces-

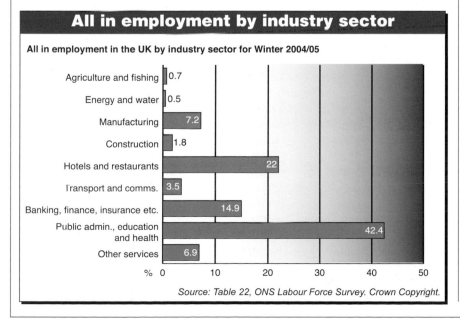

All in employment by industry sector

All in employment in the UK by industry sector for Winter 2004/05

Industry sector	%
Agriculture and fishing	0.7
Energy and water	0.5
Manufacturing	7.2
Construction	1.8
Hotels and restaurants	22
Transport and comms.	3.5
Banking, finance, insurance etc.	14.9
Public admin., education and health	42.4
Other services	6.9

Source: Table 22, ONS Labour Force Survey. Crown Copyright.

sions youth unemployment tends to rise more rapidly than adult joblessness.

The relative disadvantage of youth is more pronounced in developing countries, where they make up a strikingly higher proportion of the labour force than in industrialised economies, the report says. Eighty-five per cent of the world's youth live in developing countries and are 4.1 times more likely to be unemployed than adults, as compared to 2.3 times in industrialised economies.

The report also says that labour force participation rates for young people decreased in the world as a whole by almost four percentage points, partly as a result of young people staying in education or dropping out of the labour force. Participation was highest in East Asia (73.2 per cent) and sub-Saharan Africa (65.4 per cent) and lowest in the Middle East and North Africa (39.7 per cent).

Sub-Saharan Africa, and the Middle East and North Africa were the only regions to show a rise in the share of young people participating in labour markets. In sub-Saharan Africa, stagnation in poverty reduction is forcing all those who are able to work to take any available job, while in the Middle East and North Africa, young women are making inroads in the labour market despite the general persistence of traditional family roles.

The report says that as well as suffering from fewer chances of finding employment, young people face discrimination based on age, sex and socioeconomic background. In all regions, the inactivity rate of

young women is higher, and the employment-to-population ratios lower, than that of young men. Dominant ethnic groups fare better in most countries' job markets, and the study found that, in general, youth from lower-income households are more likely to be unemployed.

As well as suffering from fewer chances of finding employment, young people face discrimination based on age, sex and socioeconomic background

---

In developing regions – which have the largest shares of youth within the working-age population – the fate of youth entering the labour force in years to come will depend both on economic growth rates and on improvement in the employment content of growth, the report says. In industrialised economies, demographic change will likely reduce youth unemployment regions – but not automatically, the report warns. In the developing regions, as well as in the industrialised economies, a combination of both targeted and integrated policies on youth unemployment is needed to enable young people to overcome their natural disadvantage against older, more experienced workers.

Such policies have been identified by the UN Secretary-General's Youth Employment Network (YEN), a UN/World Bank/ILO partnership, headquartered at the ILO. Created following the Millennium Summit, the Network has responded to the growing challenge of youth employment by pooling the skills, experiences and knowledge of diverse partners at the global, national and local level.

The YEN has promoted the development of national action plans on youth employment among a group of 'lead countries'. So far ten countries (Note 2) have stepped forward to champion the development of national policies to showcase innovative solutions to meet the youth employment challenge.

Youth Employment Network

The Youth Employment Network (YEN), a partnership under the leadership of the heads of the UN, the World Bank and the ILO (and headquartered at the ILO) which aims to tackle the issue of youth employment at the global, national and local levels, has promoted the development of national action plans on youth employment. So far ten countries (Note 2) have stepped forward to act as 'lead countries' to champion the development of these national plans, as called for by two recent United Nations General Assembly Resolutions, (Note 4) and to showcase their experiences.

Supporting Lead Countries

The ILO is providing technical support and policy advice to countries within this partnership. Such tools include the recently released guide, *Improving prospects for young women and men in the world of work – A guide to youth employment* (Note 3), which specifies basic considerations, trade-offs and experiences which can be drawn upon to develop and implement policies, including national action plans on youth employment. Other tools include the *Global Employment Trends for Youth, 2004* which is featured in this issue of the *World of Work*, and the ILO 'School-to-Work' transition surveys (Note 5), both of which are assisting policy-makers in understanding the nature of the youth employment challenge and the views of young people today.

These kinds of tools are being used by policymakers in Indonesia, one of the lead countries. Under the direction of the Indonesia YEN (I-YEN) steering committee a National Youth Employment Action Plan for Indonesia (I-YEAP) has been drafted. This follows a major consultation process led by the I-YEN, involving the Indonesian Government, YEN core partner institutions, workers, employers, non-governmental organisations, youth, and the academic community. This Plan was publicly launched on International Youth Day – 12 August 2004 – and will form the basis of Indonesia's national action plan (NAP) on youth employment to be submitted to the UN General Assembly by September 2004.

Empowering youth

The YEN sees youth involvement in the development and implementation of these NAPs as vital for the creation of successful youth employment policy, since countries which don't adequately involve youth organisations as partners in the process risk developing policy which is divorced from realities of the problem. Lead countries are increasingly taking this message to heart:

■ In Azerbaijan, youth NGOs, led by the National Youth Council for Azerbaijan (NAYORA), have formed a coalition which will work closely with the Government to provide youth inputs into the development of Azerbaijan's NAP.

■ In Namibia, the Minister of Higher Education has invited the Namibian National Youth Council (NNYC) to assist his ministry in the creation of a task team which will work to develop the country's NAP.

At the international level the YEN has launched a Youth Consultative Group (YCG). This group will be a sounding board for YEN decision makers as well as spokespersons to represent concerns of young people on the function, direction and priorities of the YEN. They will interact with the YEN's High Level Panel of Experts providing input into YEN decision making and policy formulation.

The Group will also act as a catalyst and resource for national youth organisations looking to become involved in the NAP process. The YCG offers regional and international linkages, and provides access to information and tools, including guidelines and workshops which help assist in the effective and substantive participation of youth in employment policymaking at the national level.

Leveraging partnerships

In order to support the national action plan process, the YEN is working to create a network of networks – a community comprised of policymakers, employers and workers, young people and other stakeholders who are united in a common interest and agenda: the vital importance of youth employment as an issue within the framework of the Millennium Development Goals and poverty reduction, as well as the wider development agenda.

The relative disadvantage of youth is more pronounced in developing countries, where they make up a strikingly higher proportion of the labour force than in industrialised economies

---

Taking this multi-stakeholder approach, the YEN pools their skills and know-how of these disparate groups, leverages their accumulated experiences and resources, and identifies best practices to share, replicate, and bring to scale.

Some examples of these strategic alliances include:

■ Supporting Youth Business China (YBC), a joint initiative of Youth Business International (YBI) and the All-China Youth Federation (ACYF), which is helping young Chinese entrepreneurs succeed, through a package of assistance which includes start-up capital, business mentoring and support services.

■ Partnering with the Dräger Foundation of Germany, which has devoted its XVth Malente Symposium to youth employment, using the YEN framework to bring together 400 participants from across the social and political spectrum to examine and evaluate strategies for youth employment.

■ Encouraging and participating in tripartite meetings on youth employment and emphasising the powerful role which social dialogue has in addressing the youth employment challenge.

Notes

■ Note 1 – *Global Employment Trends for Youth, 2004*, International Labour Office, Geneva, 2004, ISBN 92-2-115997-3.

■ Note 2 – Azerbaijan, Brazil, Egypt, Indonesia, Iran, Mali, Namibia, Rwanda, Senegal and Sri Lanka.

■ Note 3 – *Improving prospects for young women and men in the world of work – A guide to youth employment*. Policy considerations and recommendations for the development of national action plans on youth employment. ILO, 2004, ISBN 92-2-115945-0.

■ Note 4 – The December 2002 Resolution on promoting youth employment (A/RES/57/165) and Resolution A/RES/58/133, of January 2004, concerning policies and programmes involving youth.

■ Note 5 – School-to-Work transition surveys have been carried out in Indonesia, Bahrain and Vietnam so far.

■ The above information is from the ILO – visit www.ilo.org or see page 41 for address details.

© *International Labour Organization 2005*

■ Having to work harder and act like 'robots', with little scope for personal initiative, are the chief reasons for declining job satisfaction in Britain, according to new research sponsored by the ESRC. (page 1)

■ Over 4 million workers, 15% of the total workforce, are dissatisfied or very dissatisfied with their jobs. (page 2)

■ Working for yourself makes you happy: more than 80% of the self-employed are satisfied or very satisfied with their jobs, while 67% of part-timers and 64% of full-timers say they are satisfied with work. (page 2)

■ Some 82% of Brits would consider working abroad, according to research released by Manpower. (page 3)

■ The UK now has the second highest proportion of men working more than 60 hours per week in the EU, with Ireland the highest. (page 6)

■ Employers fear 25 million days were lost last year through staff taking non-genuine sickness absence or 'pulling sickies'. That accounts for 15% of all absence at a cost of £1.75bn. (page 6)

■ British workers are less likely to take short-term time off sick than in any European country except Denmark; only Austria, Germany and Ireland lose less working time due to long-term absence. (page 8)

■ Companies doing badly are more likely to appoint a woman to the board – but once performance picks up, other women are less likely to be made directors. (page 9)

■ Losing a job is more traumatic than divorce or widowhood, according to a study. (page 10)

■ Just 54% of those in their 30s are happy with their work-life balance and a mere 17% are happy to work until they are 70 – the lowest numbers among all age groups. (page 14)

■ All women are entitled to 26 weeks' paid maternity leave, followed by a further 26 weeks' unpaid. (page 16)

■ Employees want work-life balance – nearly four-fifths of employees (78%) believe they should be able 'to balance their work and home lives' as they choose and 95% believe that 'people work best when they can balance their home and other aspects of their lives'. (page 16)

■ There are 7.4 million part-time workers in the UK. 78% of all part-time workers are women. (page 17)

■ Flexible hours, homeworking and special leave have helped to cut absence in both the private and public sectors. (page 18)

■ Teleworking is where some or all of the work you do for someone else is carried out in your home. (page 19)

■ Fathers are less likely to work part-time (4%) than men without children (9%), unlike mothers, who are more likely to work part-time (60%) than women without children (32%). (page 24)

■ Three-quarters of households now have dual incomes, but women still take responsibility for most of the housework, according to research funded by the ESRC. (page 26)

■ According to a recent YouGov poll of 2,000 employees, one in seven have already left the day job to go abroad, and more than 75% are thinking of doing the same. (page 27)

■ Over 90% of British workers regularly put more effort into their job than is expected of them, and over two-thirds regularly do unpaid overtime. (page 28)

■ 16- and 17-year-olds have a minimum wage of £3 per hour. The minimum wage for 18- to 21-year-olds is £4.10 per hour. (page 31)

■ The UK currently has a million people unemployed, with a further 7.6 million people of working age inactive in the labour market. (page 31)

■ Over half (52 per cent) of British companies experienced sustained difficulty in recruiting skilled staff in the last year – the highest level over the 13-year life of the Lloyds TSB Corporate Business in Britain survey. (page 31)

■ After falling in 2002 and 2003 graduate vacancies rose 15.5% last year and are expected to rise a further 14.5% this year. (page 35)

■ *Global Employment Trends for Youth, 2004* puts the global youth unemployment rate at 14.4 per cent in 2003, a 26.8 per cent increase in the total number of unemployed young people over the past decade. (page 37)

■ The industrialised world saw a notable decrease in youth unemployment in the last decade (from 15.4 per cent in 1993, to 13.4 per cent in 2003). (page 37)

ADDITIONAL RESOURCES

You might like to contact the following organisations for further information. Due to the increasing cost of postage, many organisations cannot respond to enquiries unless they receive a stamped, addressed envelope.

Chartered Institute of Personnel and Development (CIPD)
151 The Broadway
Wimbledon
LONDON SW19 1JQ
Tel: 020 8971 9000
Email: ipd@cipd.co.uk
Website: www.cipd.co.uk
With over 105,000 members it is the professional body for those involved in the management and development of people.

Confederation of British Industry (CBI)
Centre Point
103 New Oxford Street
LONDON WC1 1DU
Tel: 020 7379 7400
Website: www.cbi.org.uk
The UK's premier independent business organisation exists to ensure the government of the day, the European Commission and the wider community understand both the needs of British business and the contribution it makes to the well-being of UK society.

Economic and Social Research Council (ESRC)
Polaris House
North Star Avenue
SWINDON
Wiltshire SN2 1UJ
Tel: 01793 413000
Email: exrel@esrc.ac.uk
Website: www.esrc.ac.uk
The ESRC is the UK's largest independent funding agency for research and postgraduate training into social and economic issues.

Equal Opportunities Commission (EOC)
Arndale House, Arndale *Centre
MANCHESTER M4 3EQ
Tel: 0161 833 9244
Email: info@eoc.org.uk
Website: www.eoc.org.uk
The EOC is the leading agency working to eliminate sex discrimination in 21st-century Britain.

International Labour Organization (ILO)
Millbank Tower
21-24 Mill Bank
LONDON SW1P 4QP
Tel: 0207 828 6401
Email: london@ilo.org
Website: www.ilo.org
The International Labour Organization is the United Nations agency with global responsibility for work, employment and labour market issues.

Manpower UK Ltd
Capital Court
Windsor Street
UXBRIDGE
West Sussex UB8 1AB
Tel: 01895 205200
Email: customer.services@manpower.co.uk
Website: www.manpower.co.uk
Holds seminars, meetings exhibitions and an annual conference.

Maternity Alliance
Unit 3.3
2-6 Northburgh Street
LONDON EC1V 0AY
Tel: 020 7490 7639
Email: office@maternityalliance.org.uk
Website: www.maternityalliance.org.uk
Publishes books, reports and information leaflets for parents-to-be, returners to work, and professionals on all aspects of maternity rights and services.
Information Line: 020 7490 7638

Ufi Headquarters Sheffield Office
Learn Direct
Dearing House
1 Young Street
Sheffield S1 4UP
Tel: 0114 291 5000
Website: www.ufi.com
Ufi Ltd is the organisation responsible for learndirect, the largest government-backed supported e-learning initiative in the world, learndirect advice and UK online.

UNISON
1 Mabledon Place
LONDON WC1H 9AJ
Tel: 0845 355 0845
Website: www.unison.org.uk
UNISON is Britain's biggest trade union with over 1.3 million members. Our members are people working in the public services, for private contractors providing public services and the essential utilities. They include frontline staff and managers working full or part time in local authorities, the NHS, the police service, colleges and schools, the electricity, gas and water industries, transport and the voluntary sector.

Working Families
1-3 Berry Street
LONDON EC1V 0AA
Tel: 020 7253 7243
Email: info@www.workingfamilies.org.uk
Website: www.workingfamilies.org.uk
The voice of working parents – campaigns to improve the quality of life for working parents and their children.

The Work Foundation (formerly The Industrial Society)
Peter Runge House
3 Carlton House Terrace
LONDON SW1Y 5DG
Tel: 08701 656700
Email: contact@theworkfoundation.com
Website: www.theworkfoundation.com
The Work Foundation is an independent, not-for-profit thinktank and consultancy. Through research, campaigning and practical interventions, they aim to improve the productivity and the quality of working life in the UK.

INDEX

absenteeism 6-8, 18
accidents and injuries 8
Adams, Jenny 15
apprenticeships 36
Ashworth, Charles 7
aspirations gap 2
Azaerbaijan 39

Barber, Brendan 14, 18
Barclays 27
Beck, Ulrich 11
Behar, Darren 10
Best Boss awards 5
bosses' management styles 5
Bouley, Olivier 18
break times 30
Brennan, Clare 19-20
British Airways 27
BT 15, 20
business start-ups 4, 22

Cannon, Fiona 5
career advice 32
career breaks 27
career progression 28
caring responsibilities 17-18
childcare services 12, 16, 21, 23
    emergency childcare 22
colleagues 7
compressed hours 19
contract sales 22
Cowling, Marc 6
Cridland, John 6, 12, 13

Daley, Hope 8
Davidson, Lucy 15
Destiny, Hazel 3
Dhingra, Dolly 31-2
disabled children 21
disabled workers 12
domestic tasks 23

Economic and Social Research Council 9
education white paper 34
Edwards, Paul 27
employment service 32
entrepreneurs 4
Essex, Hannah 36
exam results 33

fathers' employment patterns 24-5
Finland 1
flexi-time 19
flexible working 2, 11-12, 14-19
    father-friendly employment 25

and new parents 16
    options for 19, 22
    right to request 17-18, 21-2
    and sickness absence 18
freelance work 22
future of work 11-13

gap years 27
gender pay gap 13, 25, 26
Georgellis, Yannis 10
Germany 1
Gilleard, Carl 35
glass cliff/glass ceiling 9
global youth unemployment 37-9
graduates 14-15, 35-6
Green, Francis 1
Griffiths, Julie 18

Haggar, Liz 15
Harkness, Susan 26
Haslam, Alex 9
Hawes, Dan 14
Hayward, Robert 15
Hendry, Ross 14
Hill, Melissa 22
Hogarth, Kevin 32
holiday entitlements 3
homeworking 12, 14-15, 19-20, 22
    and insurance 20
Hopkinson, Ian 13
hot-desking 15
hours of work 2, 3, 6, 14, 24
    maximum working hours 30-1
HSBC 13

IBM 15
incomes 2, 13
    and extra effort at work 28
    gender pay gap 13, 25, 26
    of graduates 35-6
    minimum wage 31
    and part-time working 17
injuries and accidents 8
insurance, and homeworking 20
IT and telecoms industry 5

Jackson, Sarah 5
job hunting 31-2
job satisfaction 1-2, 13
    and self-employment 2
job security 1, 2
job-sharing 19
Jones, Alexandra 11
journalism 36
Jowell, Tessa 31

Keynes, John Maynard 11
Kilner, Annabel 15

leadership 5
Learndirect 4, 32
LloydsTSB 5, 31
Loan, Erum 15
long hours culture *see* hours of work
Lusted, Dudley 7

McDowell, Linda 23
management styles 5
Manpower 3, 7, 28
manufacturing sector 7, 10
married workers 2
    see also working parents
Maternity Alliance 16
maternity leave 16, 21
maximum working hours 30-1
meal breaks 30
media industry 5
minimum wage 31
Modern Apprenticeships 36
Most Valued Employee 28
mothers' employment patterns 26

Namibia 39
Navin, Peter 33
Netherlands 1
night work 30-1
Nolan, Peter 11

Oaff, Barbara 35-6
older workers 12-13
outsourcing 13
overtime 8, 14

parental leave 21
parents *see* working parents
Parsons, Sarah 32
part-time work 17, 18, 19, 22
paternity leave 21
Porter, Gillian 27
presenteeism 6
private sector employees 7
public sector workers 7, 8, 13

qualifications 1, 34

racial integration 12
recruitment agencies 32
redundancy 10
retail industry 5
retirement age 13
Riding, Michael 31
Rifkin, Jeremy 11
Ryan, Michelle 9

safety at work 31
salaries *see* incomes
school hours working 19

school leavers 33
Scott, Benjamin 35
self-employment 2
    business start-ups 4, 22
service sector 7
Shell 15
sickness absence 6-8
    and flexible working 18
skills shortages 31-3
    education white paper 34
stress 8, 18
Stuart, Liz 11-13
students 33, 35-6

teaching jobs 36
tele-commuting 22
teleworking 19-20
    see also homeworking
term-time working 19
trade unions 31
training 4, 34
transport industry 5
Turpin, Sarah 4

unemployment 10, 37-9
unions 31
Unison 6, 8, 14
United States 1
unpaid leave 27
unpaid overtime 8, 14
Unsung Heroes competition 28

voluntary reduction in hours (V-time) 19

wages *see* incomes
Westwood, Andy 32
White, Michael 11, 12, 13
women
    employment prospects 32
    and the future of work 12
    gender pay gap 13, 25, 26
    glass cliff/glass ceiling 9
    maternity leave 16, 21
    and part-time working 17
    working mothers 26
Work Foundation 6
work-life balance 6, 14, 16
    see also hours of work
workaholism 29
working abroad 3
Working Families 5
working hours *see* hours of work
working parents 21-2
    fathers 24-5
    mothers 26
workophiles 2
workplace nurseries 12

Yorkshire Water 27
younger workers 30-1
youth unemployment 37-9

ACKNOWLEDGEMENTS

The publisher is grateful for permission to reproduce the following material.

While every care has been taken to trace and acknowledge copyright, the publisher tenders its apology for any accidental infringement or where copyright has proved untraceable. The publisher would be pleased to come to a suitable arrangement in any such case with the rightful owner.

Chapter One: Work in the UK Today

Job satisfaction?, © ESRC, *The joy of work?*, © The Work Foundation, *Auf wiedersehen, pet?*, © Manpower 2004, *Unprepared, uninformed and unsure of success*, © Ufi, *Do you work for a tyrant or a pussycat?*, © Working Families, *UK employees working longest hours in Europe*, © UNISON, *Sicknote culture?*, © Working Balance, *'Sicknote Britain' an urban myth, says TUC report*, © UNISON, *Pride and prejudice blur men's view of the glass cliff*, © ESRC, *Losing your job is 'worse than losing a loved one'*, © Associated Newspapers Ltd, *Work this way*, © Guardian Newspapers Limited.

Chapter Two: The Work-Life Balance

Workers in 30s suffer most from work-life imbalance, © UNISON, *The time and the place . . .*, © Guardian Newspapers Limited, *Flexibility for parents*, © Maternity Alliance, *Work-life balance in the British economy*, © Crown Copyright, *Part-time and flexible working*, © EOC, *Flexible working can keep your absence rates healthy*, © CIPD, *Flexible working*, © everywoman.co.uk, *What are working from home and teleworking?*, © iVillage Ltd, *Becoming a working parent*, © Opportunity Links, *Working from home*, © Melissa Hill, *Work and childcare*, © ESRC, *Facts abour working dads*, © Fathers Direct and EOC 2005, *Mothers on the run*, © ESRC, *Arranging a grown-up gap year*, © Guardian Newspapers Limited, *Working hard?*, © Manpower 2004, *Are you a workaholic?*, © handbag.com

Chapter Three: Work and Young People

Young people at work, © Trades Union Congress, *The skills gap*, © iVillage Ltd, *Skills shortage 12-year high*, © Lloyds TSB 2005, *Job crisis for school leavers*, © CIPD, *Business welcomes education white paper*, © CBI, *Is it really worth it?*, © Guardian Newspapers Limited, *Modern Apprenticeships*, © CWT, *Youth unemployment at all-time high*, © International Labour Organization.

Photographs and illustrations:

Pages 1, 20: Pumpkin House; pages 2, 17, 28: Don Hatcher; pages 3, 11, 24, 29, 35: Simon Kneebone; pages 4, 26, 39: Bev Aisbett; pages 5, 30: Angelo Madrid.

Craig Donnellan
Cambridge
September, 2005